A timely comment fro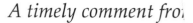

The sad death of Queen Elizabeth II occurred as this book was going to press. It is relevant to note how important Jesus was for her in strengthening the commitment to service which has won her universal accolades. Many times in her Christmas broadcasts she spoke of this, which is especially remarkable because of the consciously secular atmosphere in which we live today. Yet time and again it is people with a profound faith who have changed things — people like Mandela and Desmond Tutu and the Dalai Lama.

In his address at the Thanksgiving Service in St. Giles' Cathedral Edinburgh on September 12, 2022, the Moderator of The Church of Scotland's General Assembly, the Rt. Revd. Dr. Iain Greenshields, spoke of her sharp intellect and breadth of understanding of world affairs. Without doubt the Queen's Christian faith was genuine when she spoke unashamedly of the example and teaching of Jesus Christ whom she strove to follow as best she could.

Her faith can nevertheless easily be interpreted in childish terms as this article in *The Times* (Sept. 9, 2022, p.47) seems to suggest: "Her faith was based not on intellectual curiosity nor theological speculation but on the simple verities she learnt as a child, which she neither questioned nor challenged."

Discussion after the death of Prince Philip made it clear that he had a strong intellectual interest in discovering the truth about Christianity. He was no mere passive listener to sermons but would actively debate what was said in them. It is highly unlikely that the Queen did not share in his spirit of candid enquiry.

I hope that my book may help to dispel any anti-intellectual approach to Christian commitment, and provide an opportunity for widespread debate.

What are people saying about

The Jesus Puzzle

This is an important book. Brenda Watson's close analysis of arguments of scholarly sceptics is convincing. Her writing is sharp and engaging, drawing the reader into recent and not so recent debates about the historical existence of Jesus and why it matters. It is both passionate and clear, forcing the sceptics into a corner and challenging them to respond. Will there be a fightback? RE teachers will find here both a summary of scholarship and a critique of it. The book will help many to consider the Gospels and remind us of the powerful influence of Christianity over Western civilisation, an influence often neglected or forgotten.

Penny Thompson, a former teacher and freelance researcher who has written extensively about Religious Education in schools

The Jesus Puzzle rigorously examines principles underlying Quests for the historical Jesus, and exposes preconceptions that impede understanding. It robustly challenges dogmatisms, both secular and religious, commending open-mindedness and a combination of reason and faith, as of cognition and emotional awareness. It argues in favour of the overall historicity of the gospels and against an a priori rejection of the supernatural, accepting that all our knowledge is provisional. The book emphasises the relevance of the human Jesus for today with his message of putting people first. I am happy to commend Brenda Watson's book as a thought-provoking and balanced study of historical method coupled with comprehensive awareness of the centrality of Jesus in Western thought and culture. Her discussion of the Resurrection is particularly illuminating.

The Revd Nicholas Menon, a former University and School Chaplain

A book which deserves to be read by anyone who imagines that a modern, liberal approach to Christian faith has to be based on extreme scepticism, particularly about the Gospel accounts of Jesus. Not all will agree with every one of her conclusions, but her arguments – drawn as much from the philosophy of history and of science as from theology – demand serious attention from the "cultured despisers" of faith in our own time. **Anthony Woollard MA BD STM**, a Trustee of Modern Church (a leading theological society promoting open-minded thinking about Christian faith) and editor of its newsletter *Signs of the Times*

As a committed agnostic or scientific atheist, I think that Jesus existed and taught, so that Western Civilization has not been deluded. He and his have rightly become the principal subjects of our art, our architecture, our literature and our music, a place established and maintained on the historical basis of His words and deeds. Watson does not shrink from contrasting the violent and political practice of so-called Christianity through the ages from the benign teaching of Jesus himself, the "gospel of love".

This study is timely. Books about His work are particularly important at this time when the World is crying out for clear moral leadership towards a life of peace, health and prosperity based on recent advances in technology. Given such leadership, Science and Christ's teaching can now advance hand-in-hand to solve existing problems and better the human condition. But it is sad that so many competent technologists seem incapable of profiting from Jesus' moral teaching, preferring to set themselves up as personal saviours of mankind through their often spurious inventions such as the "carbon footprint".

It is possible that some Jesus teaching, not least about the miracles, is the work of later authors but this is probably crucial only for professional historians. Watson's review of the history is scholarly and well-referenced, especially her spirited defence of the "resurrection story", but I personally believe that "concern for evidence" should remain subsidiary to moral guidance either as His most credible direct speech or through the parable examples.

Derek Smith, Professor of Materials at Queen Mary University of London, Director of the Industrial Materials Research Unit, Chairman of QMC Instruments, Chairman of QMC Advanced Technology

In the first chapter of John's Gospel one reads: "In the beginning was the Word ... And the Word was made flesh, and dwelt among us." This in essence is the Christian teaching about the incarnation. The transcendent God, who is wholly or entirely other, and hence unknown, is in fact made known in the created world but very specifically in this one, singular life, Jesus. If there is even a modicum of truth in this Christian teaching one would expect not only a serious intellectual interest in coming to understand the natural world but also a passionate intellectual interest in history, and specifically in the history of this one particular life.

Brenda Watson in her book *The Jesus Puzzle*, coolly and passionately rational, takes up the challenge of showing intellectually that we can come to know the past generally, and this life of Jesus in particular. She does this in the face of the widespread historical scepticism to be found in the modern world. She writes accessibly, without obfuscation, about the available evidence that would give real world substance to a core Christian belief. It may not be possible to deduce the key claims of faith directly from claims about the empirical world or about the past, but it is the case that religious beliefs are grounded and tested there. In brief, the affirmations of faith can be falsified by the past. It is this vulnerability to historical investigation which also gives these affirmations their weight and power. Christianity is not a theory or a world view but a way of life that is rationally and historically informed. This book, *The Jesus Puzzle*, makes a timely contribution to make this more evident in our sceptical age.

Dr Marius C. Felderhof, Honorary Senior Research Fellow, Department of Theology and Religion, The University of Birmingham, UK

Are accounts of Jesus' life mere 'stories' or based on historical fact? Is that relevant for faith? This incisive and important book argues — against the lazy prejudices of the present age — that what really happened nearly two thousand years ago still does matter. It deserves to be widely read.

Professor Roger Trigg, Senior Research Fellow, Ian Ramsey Centre, University of Oxford, Emeritus Professor of Philosophy at the University of Warwick

The Jesus Puzzle

Challenging Intellectual
Uncertainty About Jesus

The Jesus Puzzle

Challenging Intellectual
Uncertainty About Jesus

Brenda Watson

CHRISTIAN ALTERNATIVE
BOOKS

Winchester, UK
Washington, USA

JOHN HUNT PUBLISHING

First published by Christian Alternative Books, 2022
Christian Alternative Books is an imprint of John Hunt Publishing Ltd.,
No. 3 East St., Alresford, Hampshire SO24 9EE, UK
office@jhpbooks.com
www.johnhuntpublishing.com
www.christian-alternative.com

For distributor details and how to order please visit the 'Ordering' section on our website.

Text copyright: Brenda Watson 2021

ISBN: 978 1 80341 012 8
978 1 80341 013 5 (ebook)
Library of Congress Control Number: 2021949959

A CIP catalogue record for this book is available from the British Library.

Design: Matthew Greenfield

UK: Printed and bound by CPI Group (UK) Ltd, Croydon, CR0 4YY
Printed in North America by CPI GPS partners

We operate a distinctive and ethical publishing philosophy in
all areas of our business, from our global network of authors to
production and worldwide distribution.

Contents

Introduction   1

Chapter 1 Does it Matter that We Know
     about Jesus Today?   3

Chapter 2 The Scholarly Quests for the
     Historical Jesus   14

Chapter 3 The Nature of History   27

Chapter 4 Giving Initial Benefit of Doubt:
     1st Historical Principle   41

Chapter 5 The Impact of Failure to Observe
     Initial Benefit of Doubt   53

Chapter 6 The Uniqueness of Historical Events:
     2nd Historical Principle   67

Chapter 7. Explanation of Major Facts: 3rd
     Historical Principle   80

Chapter 8 The Problem of Non-Explanation   94

Chapter 9 Overcoming the Reason/Faith Dichotomy   107

Appendix Further Information about the
     Scholarly Quests   113

References   118

To Meriel without whose constant encouragement and support this book would never have been written.

Also by Brenda Watson

Education and Belief (Blackwell 1987). ISBN: 9780631152088

Truth and Scripture (Aureus 2004).
ISBN, 1899750274

The Effective Teaching of Religious Education 2nd. Edition with
Penny Thompson (Pearson/Longman 2007).
ISBN: 9781405824101

Making Education Fit for Democracy: Closing the Gap
(Routledge 2020).
ISBN: 9780367220372

"An Unbelievable Myth: The Invention of Jesus?" *Think* 50:17
Autumn 2018.
IBSN: 1477–1756

Acknowledgements

I have received much help from discussion with many people. Those most closely involved to whom I give my sincere personal thanks are: Dr. Elizabeth Ashton for supportive reading of chapters, many helpful suggestions, and much illuminating discussion. Meriel Bennett for proofreading, plentiful help in reading of chapters, and thoughtful engagement with the book throughout. Stuart Freed for final formatting of the text. Derek Smith and David Watson for valuable discussion and reading of chapters.

Introduction

This book concerns taking the earthly life of Jesus seriously.

First, as a modest attempt to challenge the assumed atheism of our times in its dismissal of the importance of Jesus.

Christianity is widely assumed to be based on a fairy story which can be discarded. It treats the Gospels as unreliable documents from a pre-scientific, superstitious world, for which we have no use today. They were written only as propaganda.

This scepticism concerning the gospels is presumed to rely on reason when it is in fact irrational. For the question of how Christianity emerged at all if the gospels are discounted as historically suspect is largely ignored, or given a number of purely conjectural explanations without any strong historical evidence for them at all.

The so-called Quest for the historical Jesus still fascinates scholars and claims to be historical enquiry, but it has in practice been mired in ideology, whether religious or anti-religious; it has often discounted basic historical principles. Jesus of Nazareth was a real human being living at a precise time and amenable to investigation by anyone because he was part of the public world of nature and history. He was not just a figure in which Christians have invested a huge amount of manufactured faith.

Second, as an attempt to encourage Christians to take the gospels more seriously as historical material for the life of Jesus.

It is sad, and also incoherent, to believe in Jesus as fully human as well as fully divine, and not to try to get as close a historically responsible understanding of him as a human being as possible. The gospels tend to be regarded by some Christians as just devotional material to be read in church in extracts without concern for their historical context.

Questions about what Jesus really taught and did should not be ignored. If they are, there is a danger that the Bible becomes almost idolized as a supreme authority which cannot be challenged or conceived mistaken in any way. Phrases such as "The Bible says..." are still common, treating the Bible as *the* Word of God as though there can be no other. This tendency goes back quite early in the Church's history and was promoted even more by the Reformation which pitted the Bible against appeal to papal authority.

This attitude has created a great and unnecessary divide between faith and rational enquiry. It has further promoted a use of the Bible for "proof-texts" to bolster support for current controversies. So it has been, and still is, responsible for much un-Christian in-fighting and has served to distract attention from Jesus as a human being. The modern controversies over the role of women, gender etc., still see people quoting particular passages from Scripture in an exceedingly un-historical manner.

The question concerning what we can reliably know about Jesus as a human being has, however, been bedevilled by much misunderstanding. It is the purpose of this book to try to shed light on this quest.

Chapter 1

Does It Matter That We Know About Jesus Today?

A strange amnesia

A strange amnesia appears to have overtaken the West. It has almost completely lost touch with the world view which has made it so distinctive and contributed so much to the values it both consciously and unconsciously holds. It has become common practice simply to ignore 2000 years of Christianity as though the Enlightenment appeared from nowhere or simply from insights gleaned from the Graeco-Roman world. Any mention of religion and specifically of Christianity contributing anything of value to Western civilisation is mostly masked out of the picture.

In reading for my recent book *Making Education Fit for Democracy* (2021), I was struck by the almost complete omission of any reference to the Christian institutions from which the schools and universities of the West emerged. It almost seemed as though education sprang up as something new following the Enlightenment, and the Industrial Revolution in its wake, which required people to be educated up to at least basic levels.

A typical example at an everyday level of over-looking Christianity is how the Christmas Books Catalogue for 2019, drawn up by the Booksellers Association, had hardly any books on religion. It was presumed that Christmas is a secular festival. What about the millions of people who happily choose to sing carols at Christmas? Well, the words seemingly don't matter at all; faith in Jesus may as well be no more than faith in Santa Claus; we grow out of both. We can enjoy singing carols in a sentimental/nostalgic way and appreciate the camaraderie of the Christmas season, but the stories are just incidental. Christmas was, after all, a pagan festival of mid-winter before

Christianity came along.

It is significant that a highly-reviewed publication such as *The Week*, which advertises itself as giving "All you need to know about everything that matters", has no section on religion at all. It carries a wide range of topics from politics to sport, consumer information to the arts, business to media, but readers are presumed to have no interest in Christianity or any other religion.

This does not appear to be the case when, for example, Dan Brown's 2003 mystery novel, *The Da Vinci Code*, could become "The Greatest Story Ever Sold", mocking the title of the 1965 American film *The Greatest Story Ever Told*. As is well established, the content of the novel is a hoax, yet its vague presumption of truth effectively took huge numbers of people in. This suggests that, though mostly unacknowledged, Christianity is still very much present in the popular psyche.

Amongst intellectuals, however, there is little acknowledgement of the importance of Christianity. Articles like Raphael Lataster's in the philosophy journal *Think* (2016) indeed argue that we can now rationally doubt even the historical existence of Jesus. Julian Baggini begins his chapter in Tom Holland's book *Revolutionary* with the words "No one really knows who Jesus was, what he said and did, or even whether he really existed" (2020, p.152). Jesus quite possibly never actually lived at all. His presumed teaching, life and death, and quite clearly his supposed resurrection, are no more than the figments of imagination by pre-scientific, pre-modern folk who have nothing to say to us today.

How can we account for this amnesia?

There are huge numbers of factors to do with the extraordinary changes the world has seen in recent centuries. These have seemed to leave older beliefs and values behind in the past, encouraging people to focus only on the present and the future. I think, however, that there is more to it than that. It reflects considerable anger with Christianity though, interestingly enough, not actually with Jesus.

Jesus is one of the few personal names understood widely throughout the world without the need to add an adjective or surname – people such as Napoleon, Hitler, Gandhi or Mandela. By itself that may mean little. What is odd, however, is that Jesus refers to someone who lived nearly 2000 years ago in a minor province of the vast Roman Empire, who never had political or military power, was unsupported by wealth, growing up in a conservative-looking rural semi-literate community beside an obscure inland lake, who collected a band of followers from amongst working people such as fishermen. He apparently preached a gospel of love and had his moment of glory being acclaimed by crowds before dying a criminal's death at the hands of the political and religious authorities of his day. Why should anyone ever have heard of him?

The likeliest reason which most people might give is because he founded a new religion called Christianity. In time this religion, though starting in an unpromising way, became powerful: an important contender on the world stage succeeding a decrepit Roman Empire and providing the substance and structure for a new civilization in the West which was able to spread its influence around the globe especially through its developing science and technology.

Rescuing Jesus from the trappings of Christianity

Perceptions of Christianity have given Jesus much bad publicity. We need to ask whether the religion synonymous with his name is what he envisaged? Is it the case that the formalism, institutionalism, hierarchy, patriarchalism and sometimes wealth of the Christian church through the ages have been at all plausibly what Jesus intended? Is it not rather that, born a Jew, he wished for the reform of his own religion in such a way that it could be made open and available for all, based on the radical simplicity of learning to love as God loves every human being? Jesus wished to point humanity in a new direction, away from a self-centred approach to living towards a life of selfless love.

If this is what historically Jesus had in mind, then those aspects of Church theory and practice over the centuries which deny such a straightforward focus on love constitute abuse of a grave kind. It is probably the case that the majority of those who are antagonistic to Christianity are such because of the failings of the Church to live up to the teaching which, despite distortions, has remained at the heart of its message. Their proper enemy is institutional Christianity not Jesus. They are likely to agree with Mahatma Gandhi's comment: "I like your Christ; I do not like your Christians. Your Christians are so unlike your Christ." Indeed, it is interesting that usually mention of Jesus commands some respect even by diehard atheists who do thus distinguish between Jesus and the religion that bears his name. Richard Dawkins once commented: "Somebody as intelligent as Jesus would have been an atheist" (You-Tube, 27 Oct 2011).

Thomas Paine, whose inspired writing was partly responsible for the American War of Independence, wrote vividly for the rest of his life in support of reason and the Enlightenment. He hated the Christian church, yet in his Age of Reason he exempted from his attack Jesus himself:

"Nothing that is here said can apply, even with the most distant disrespect, to the real character of Jesus Christ. He was a virtuous and an amiable man. The morality that he preached and practised was of the most benevolent kind; and though similar systems of morality had been preached by Confucius, and by some of the Greek philosophers, many years before; by the Quakers since, and by many good men in all ages, it has not been exceeded by any."

He clearly distinguished Jesus from Christianity: "The church has set up a system of religion very contradictory to the character of the person whose name it bears. It has set up a religion of pomp and of revenue in pretended imitation of a person whose life was humility and poverty."

If it is difficult to find anti-Jesus quotes. it is much more difficult to find any positive reference to him in major books about the intellectual history of the West. Peter Watson's book *A Terrible Beauty: A History of the People and Ideas that Shaped the Modern Mind* (2000) has a tiny reference to Jesus and largely fragmented and negative references to Christianity. Harold Bloom's *The Western Canon: the Books and School of the Ages* (1994) never mentions Jesus.

In this book I want to examine what view of Jesus can historically stand up to the rigours of genuine scholarship and enquiry. The argument I want to present does not rest on wishful thinking but on what rationally can be said to make sense regarding what we really can know historically about Jesus the man.

Why knowledge about Jesus as a human being matters

It is necessary to set Jesus apart and seek afresh the story of his earthly life from an historical perspective for at least three major reasons:

First, Jesus was a historical person who deserves to be discussed in his own right, and not given a persona by centuries of particular pro-Christian or anti-Christian views. Historical evidence concerning who he was, what he taught and how he lived and what he died for, is owed to him as to any other historical person. Yet, as the next chapter will develop, strong ideological commitments have seriously coloured the way in which Jesus has been researched.

Second, it is by no means historically certain that Jesus' purpose in life was to start a new religion. Rather, was he not concerned to renew and reform the religion of Israel enabling it to embrace the Gentiles also? The main focus of his teaching was the gospel of love – belonging to an inner kingdom of true worship of God in spirit and in truth. It was not focussed on external institutions with their inevitable distractions and stress on power and authority and "correct" external behaviour.

The parable of the Good Samaritan is highly significant. Following a question concerning what is true religion, Jesus told a story of the power of a common humane reaction to the suffering of another person. This was in contrast with the uselessness of representatives of official religion. Moreover, the true worshipper of God depicted in the story was a Samaritan – regarded then by many as not a proper Jew at all but someone whom most would shun.

Third, the failings of Christianity have so impressed people since the time of the Enlightenment that the good which Christianity did has tended to become overlooked. Thus, today in the secular West even the role of Christianity in building up the civilization of the West seems to have become largely ignored or forgotten. It may be the case that in the long history of Christianity in power the gospel of love became a casualty under a weight of political, social, financial and administrative concerns. This offers, however, no excuse for dismissing Christianity per se. The authentic understanding which Jesus taught, lived and died for has never lacked witness over the centuries, and remains the touchstone against which the achievement of Christianity can and must be measured. The crimes committed in the name of Christianity represent abuse of what Christianity stands for; they are therefore self-correcting as being the opposite of what Christians claim they do, which is to follow Jesus.

The importance of understanding about Jesus in a secular age

It may seem nevertheless that Jesus has become redundant, and should be allowed in a secular age to recede into the obscurity out of which he came. This book argues not so for several reasons. Rather, it is important that the record is put straight regarding Jesus.

(i) Knowledge and understanding matter and should displace misunderstanding, fake news, ignorance and false thinking. The cynical note of the times, which purports to suspect that there is bias and prejudice everywhere, cannot sustain a civilization. We do need to seek for the truth about what is said, what is believed, what happens and what ought to happen. A literally post-truth society cannot survive because it implies the absence of trust in people and in what they say and do.

(ii) The enormous problems associated with the twenty-first century at personal, social, national and global levels mean that the teaching of Jesus is supremely relevant today. It is not at all clear that the modern world and future do not need the input and stimulus which Jesus had to offer. The gospel of love that he preached is as powerful, relevant and enduring today in the twenty-first century as it was during his lifetime. The Covid-19 pandemic has powerfully indicated this for many people who realise that the power to endure depends on more than science can provide. Trusting in what its technology can achieve is dependent on trusting the people who use it – on their values and priorities. The modern world does not like to admit it, but self-centredness is a damaging emotion affecting everyone regardless of their position in society. Indeed, those most privileged, and those who wield most power and influence, are especially prone to its onslaught. As Lord Acton famously noted "Power corrupts, and absolute power corrupts absolutely." There are very few people who do not succumb to enjoying, in Shakespeare's pregnant phrase, "being dressed in a little brief authority."

(iii) The West has rightly emphasised the importance for each individual to have freedom to choose how she or he shall live life. What has tended to be overlooked is the degree to which people so often are not free to choose. Pressures put upon them by others in their immediate environment, by the media including today especially social media, and by the sheer force of the Zeitgeist of the times, make such thinking for oneself incredibly difficult. Moreover, ignorance of alternatives and other possibilities makes a mockery of anyone's capacity for choice. Encouragement to think outside the box is therefore most important; thinking about Jesus can certainly do that. For to show any interest or commitment to Christian values runs the risk today in the West of being counter-cultural. It is important therefore that people have access to this.

(iv) In the modern world religion continues to play a significant, indeed perhaps crucial, role. Authentic knowledge of Jesus can help people understand religion better, as well as contributing powerfully to the proper dialogue between religions which global responsibility requires. Lack of respect for the religion most closely associated with one's own culture bodes ill for appreciating the importance of religion in a very different culture. This has been demonstrated many times in the general attitude of the West towards Islam. Instead of Muslim newcomers being warmly welcomed they have met much suspicion; little sympathetic appreciation of what religion means to them has been shown.

More should be said about this because the peace of the world may depend upon it. Lack of any spirit of generosity towards what Muslims believe has not helped them to discredit the enormous threat of violent extremism in their midst. Respectful enquiry into what true belief in Allah involves is crucially needed. Non-Muslims should encourage that to take place. Instead, however, a common attitude is voiced that there is no point in such debate because of the huge gulf between reason and faith; anything said about religion is just a matter of personal opinion impervious to any proper evaluation. By learning discernment between Christianity and Jesus, the West would be in a better position to encourage the same spirit of discernment amongst the followers of other religions.

In sum, the teaching of Jesus, and the way his life reflected that teaching, is endlessly interesting, indeed fascinating. It furnishes strong arguments for the values foundational for civilized society. In discovering these, it can accommodate an enjoyable detective interest as well as offer meditative material for reflection. As Richard Tarnas puts it in *The Passion of the Western Mind: Understanding the Ideas that have Shaped our World View*: "Christianity has presided over Western cultures for most of the latter's presence, not only bearing its central spiritual impulses for two millennia but also influencing its philosophical and scientific revolution well on through the Renaissance and the Enlightenment. Even now, in less obvious but no less significant ways, the Christian world view still affects – indeed, permeates – the Western cultural psyche, even when the latter is most apparently secular in disposition" (1991, p. 91).

Why reliable knowledge of Jesus is important to counteract secularism

The status of religion in the West generally is today low. Belief in God is almost assumed to be mistaken, redundant, perhaps quaint but certainly old-fashioned and inappropriate for the modern world.

A major cause of this state of affairs is the increasing scepticism of leading intellectuals, going back well over two and half centuries. The assumption that because reason by itself cannot prove the existence of God, and therefore that "God" is only an imaginary human construct, has been powerfully at work in universities and has therefore slowly influenced everyone who has been through the education systems of the West.

The intellectual case against religion and specifically against Christianity is an aspect neglected by many Christians. This is partly because of anxiety about engaging with intellectual questions: people don't feel able to cope. The reasons for the decline of Christianity are many. They include the incredible rate of change and especially the sheer distraction of life. There is understandably enormous emphasis today on improving the prospects for living a long, healthy and happy life in this world made possible by science. Moreover, the shortcomings of religion have been widely and effectively on display, as noted above. A simple faith in Jesus has provided no guarantee against huge injustice and even violence committed in the name of Jesus.

Another set of reasons relate to the difficulty today of people even hearing what Christianity is really about. It has become politically correct to avoid any mention of religion; as Alastair Campbell famously told Blair: "We don't do God." Religious Education in British schools has had to fight for its life, and in order to survive has often become more an outsider's view of religion than one which treats truth-questions seriously, helping people to learn to think with heart and mind about religion. The result is gross ignorance generally. This provides no helpful basis for people taking religious faith seriously. All that most people have to work on tends to be rather negative stereotypes.

Yet the assumptions lying behind Paine's account are still with us today and need challenging in everyday conversation as well as by academics. Raphael Lataster, writing in the philosophy journal

Think, states this: "The Gospels are anonymous, make supernatural claims, contain ahistorical information, and are heavily influenced by the Old Testament and much earlier mythical stories. And like the Pauline Epistles the Gospels are not contemporaneous to Jesus' life and are not penned by eyewitnesses. Paul's epistles present even more challenges as there are indications that what he is discussing is purely a visionary and divine Christ rather than a historical Jesus" (2015, p. 65).

Richard Carrier, an American historian and philosopher, considers: "All we have are uncritical pro-Christian devotional or hagiographic texts filled with dubious claims written decades after the fact by authors who never tell us their methods or sources. Multiple attestation can never gain traction on such a horrid body of evidence" (2014, p. 140).

Less flamboyant – but the legacy is still there – is Karen Armstrong: "We know very little about Jesus. The first full-length account of his life was St Mark's gospel, which was not written until about the year 70, some forty years after his death. By that time, historical facts had been overlaid with mythical elements which expressed the meaning Jesus had acquired for his followers" (1993, p. 79).

The dismissal of the gospels as simply unreliable evidence is an important plank in the secularist argument. The actual question which needs to be asked, however, by those who claim to be rational is simply how true is that assessment. The rest of this book seeks to tackle that question from the point of view of the nature of historical enquiry and how the gospels should be approached to yield reliable information concerning Jesus.

Chapter 2

The Scholarly Quests for the Historical Jesus

For well over 250 years scholars have been looking into the question of what we can reliably know about Jesus as a historical person. Albert Schweitzer first called Jesus research a quest in his book with that title published in 1906.

To reach a historically reliable account of Jesus, the gospels in the New Testament provide the obvious and clear starting point. They purport to record the life of Jesus. They give four separate accounts, though three of them are clearly related. The four gospels remain distinctively different, however, in the emphasis they give. So they do acknowledge diversity which can aid the historian in seeking to understand who Jesus was.

The reliability of the gospels has, however, been subject to derision by many intellectuals, as already quoted in Chapter 1. This note of suspicion towards them has affected how the scholarly quest for the historical Jesus has been pursued. A common attitude has been that it is for the gospels to prove themselves before anything they say can be considered historically reliable. This kind of approach has affected even Christian scholars, for they have been operating within an environment that questions any religious viewpoint as no more than wish fulfilment. Drawn into discussion with other scholars, they have found themselves much on the defensive.

It is my intention in this book to challenge this sceptical starting point for discovering about who Jesus as a human person was. I ask why the gospels are approached with such caution. They are historical documents which have survived the vicissitudes of two millennia. That is remarkable in itself. Other documents from the classical world are not automatically treated with such suspicion. On the contrary, they are eagerly interrogated for what we today can learn from them.

The basic reason for suspicion of the gospels may well be the secularist surge which has hit the West like a tsunami. But there is much more to say. A crucial claim of the questers has been that they are approaching the gospels from a historical point of view and not from the perspective of religious beliefs. The secularist world view has, however, affected how historical investigation itself is seen. Empirical evidence which excludes any consideration of anything transcendent to that has been taken as the norm. This necessarily affects how historical study of any religious material is approached.

The first quest

The German scholar Hermann Samuel Reimarus (1694–1768) is generally regarded as the key thinker who kick-started this quest. His work on Jesus was published posthumously in 1778 by his friend Gottfried Lessing. They were both enthusiastic supporters of the Enlightenment; their guiding principle was reason which abandoned any dependence on religious faith. Lessing indeed used a very apt analogy to describe the impact on thinking which such Enlightenment commitment involved. There is "a big dirty ditch" separating nature and super-nature: we live in the real world of nature; the other world is an imaginary one. They were Deists who did not deny belief in God but considered all revealed religion as false.

Based on this world view, Reimarus was able to ride a coach and horses through the gospels, discounting every reference to anything supernatural such as miracles. This left very little of historical certainty. He saw Jesus as a would-be but failed earthly liberator hoping to free the Jews from the Roman yoke.

The most outstanding figure to follow Reimarus was the scholar/clergyman David Strauss whose immensely long book on the life of Jesus was translated into English by the novelist

George Eliot in 1846. It proved to be highly controversial. The Earl of Shaftesbury called the English translation "the most pestilential book ever vomited out of the jaws of hell."

Why did Strauss attract such notoriety? He basically followed Reimarus in arguing that none of the miraculous element in the gospels was historically true. He refused to defend miracles on rational grounds such as presuming that the disciples thought they saw Jesus walking on the water, when he was in fact walking on submerged rocks which they couldn't see. Instead, Strauss saw the miraculous stories in terms of myth invented by the early Church to explain how Jesus was the long-awaited Jewish Messiah.

The first Quest produced a great many lives of Jesus which conspicuously failed to convince a majority of scholars. So many of these purported lives of Jesus seemed to be more autobiographical than about Jesus! Despite his firm Christian belief, Schweitzer came to the conclusion that there was no way forward for this search. His summary has often been quoted:

"He comes to us as One unknown, without a name, as of old, by the lakeside. He came to those who knew Him not. He speaks to us the same word: 'Follow thou me!' and set us to the tasks which He has to fulfill for our time. He commands. And to those who obey Him, whether they be wise or simple, He will reveal Himself in the toils, the conflicts, the sufferings which they shall pass through in His fellowship, and, as an ineffable mystery, they shall learn in their own experience, who He is" (*The Quest of the Historical Jesus*, 1910).

But of course, Schweitzer, did not mean that Jesus was totally unknowable. He was sure, for example, that in founding his famous hospital in Lambarene in French Equatorial Africa he was fulfilling the teaching of Jesus himself. His words sprang not just from frustration at the muddle which scholars could make but also from his deep awareness of the imponderable nature of what is to be known. As he said in *The Spiritual Life* (1947), the highest knowledge is to know we are surrounded by mystery. This is something which the devotees of reason found, and still find, difficult to accept.

The second quest

The Quests are generally divided into three, Schweitzer bringing to a close the first one. Radically changing circumstances in Europe, especially in Germany, following WWI and the rise of Nazism, eventually produced a second Quest. The key figure here was Rudolf Bultmann – the most influential professor of New Testament studies of his times until his retirement in 1951 after 30 years at the University of Marburg. He was a brilliant and innovative thinker. His students included many leading theologians. He also taught the celebrated philosopher Hannah Arendt.

He became famous for his existentialist approach to theology which reflected his friendship with the philosopher Heidegger. According to this, what matters is how we live moment by moment, and for the Christian this means living by faith in Jesus Christ. This emphasis enabled him and his large number of followers to survive the disturbing and distraught times in which they lived. Bultmann was himself a member of the Confessing Church which opposed Hitler.

He has a dual importance in the history of the Quest. Firstly, He was the pioneer of the Form Critical approach to gospel studies which continued to hold the respect of scholars up to the 1960s. His important work *History of the Synoptic Tradition* (1921), took its inspiration from subjecting literary texts to investigation as to how they came to be in their final form, and therefore what their original form must have been. It analysed writings in terms of ancient literary forms and oral traditions such as love poems, parables, and proverbs. It set out to unearth the earliest form of the narrative units, termed pericopes, which came to form the gospels. Bultmann explained that the aim of Form Criticism is: "to determine the original form of a piece of narrative, a dominical saying or a parable. In the process we learn to distinguish secondary additions and forms, and these in turn lead to important results for the history of the tradition"(in *Mournet*, 2005, p. 56).

One of Bultmann's students, Ernst Kasemann, is credited with beginning the second quest in 1953 with a lecture entitled "The Problem of the Historical Jesus". He considered that, although the gospels may be interpreted for theological purposes, they still contain historical memories which can yield information about Jesus. These can be discerned if the tools of historical analysis are applied in a systematic manner. One such tool he invented was the criterion of dissimilarity that compares a gospel passage (e.g., a statement by Jesus) with the Jewish context of the time, and if dissimilar, places weight on its being authentically what Jesus said or did.

Such an approach inspired a number of scholars to research the historical Jesus along similar lines. One of the influential works that followed was Günther Bornkamm's 1956 book *Jesus of Nazareth*; he was optimistic, considering that what the gospels report concerning the message, the deeds and the history of Jesus is still distinguished by an authenticity; these features point us directly to the earthly figure of Jesus. Another influential book was by the American scholar James M. Robinson; his *A New Quest for the Historical Jesus*, (1959) was reprinted numerous times.

Secondly, however, Bultmanm is famous for a quite different approach to the gospels – what he terms the need for "de-mythologizing" them. He assumed that they were basically mythical writings not to be taken literally in any scientific sense of the word. Bultmann's emphasis on the New Testament as myth recalls the viewpoint of David Strauss in the First Quest.

Bultmann is re-positioning myth as what does not fit into a

scientific way of thinking. This is Lessing's ditch all over again. This time, however, myth was understood to be utterly true; he embraced it from the point of view of a committed Churchman. Bultmann, so far from intending to discredit the gospels as Reimarus and Lessing did, thought he was giving them the status they really have. Indeed, this was part of his missionary strategy. He believed that otherwise Christianity would be seen as irrelevant in the modern world formed by science. He considered that now all of our thinking is irrevocably formed by science.

Such dependence on science did not worry Bultmann in that he was certain that what matters is simply the believer's faith. This caused him eventually to minimise the importance of what happened regarding Jesus' historical life. Although his early work had inspired the second quest, his later work virtually brought it to an end. He became convinced that the gospels should be de-mythologized, replacing supernatural references with universal human references.

What he did not appreciate was that faith itself needs a concern for truth to distinguish it from make-belief. Bultmann's late position was summarised by him as all that matters is the "that-ness", not the "what-ness" of Jesus, i.e., only that Jesus existed, preached, and died by crucifixion matters, not what happened throughout his life. Yet "that-ness" implies fact, and how is that to be established – only through science? In the end this line of thinking would undermine any historical work on the gospels as misplaced.

The apparently objective nature of the Form Critical approach, together with the search for criteria to evaluate the gospels, also came to be viewed with suspicion, and reliance on faith seen as more like credulity. Thus, the second quest tended to fade away until revived by other factors with a very different emphasis. Bultmann in particular came in for a lot of criticism. John Meier made the interesting comment that Bultmann had a disconcerting way of solving problems with a few evasive sentences; his arguments do not hold up, despite having been handed down for generations (1991).

The third quest

Uncertainty regarding the validity of these principles and tools for critical analysis, together with a series of impressive archaeological finds and a deeper awareness of what it meant for Jesus to be Jewish, have prompted a third quest. Thus, material from the Dead Sea Scrolls forced scholars to realise the level of diversity in first-century Judaism. The context in which Jesus operated could now be seen in a much more nuanced way.

Many massive excavations in Palestine and the Roman world generally have hugely added to knowledge of the world in which Jesus lived. Increasing materials from archaeological digs etc., are enabling scholars, more fully than was possible earlier, to understand and appreciate the background for his life. As an example of this trend, Rosemary Margaret Luff suggests that: "There was considerable discontent in early 1st century Palestine. While the Galilean lower classes were not as hard-pressed as those of Judea, nevertheless there was a demand for a leader that would alleviate the suffering of the poor" (2019, p. 197).

Finds such as the synagogue at Migdal, site of Magdala, the ancient fishing city that was home to Mary Magdalene, have served to confirm what the nineteenth-century French theologian and explorer Ernest Renan hoped for: "the striking agreement of the texts with the places." Many discoveries are supporting what the gospels say. For example, in 1968, the discovery of Yehohanan's heel showed that a crucified man from Jesus' day could have been permitted Jewish burial by the Romans.

Greatly increased knowledge of first-century Palestine has therefore become possible permitting an emphasis on Jesus as Jewish which had often not been properly highlighted before. A new generation of scholars are determined to put Jesus properly into the context of his times. In 1977 an important work by E.P. Sanders, *Paul and Palestinian Judaism*, renewed interest in the historical Jesus. A number of scholars presented new approaches within a relatively short time of each other, and so in 1982, Tom Wright coined the term "third quest" to refer to these.

Explicit attention to the Jewishness of Jesus became a particular trend, noting especially the work of the Jewish historian Géza Vermes. His widely publicised books, written in an accessible style, have deservedly commanded much attention.

The third quest is promoting optimism among many scholars. Wright wrote in 1998: "Fortified by the Jewish materials now more readily available, these scholars worked as historians, under no doubt that it is possible to know quite a lot about Jesus of Nazareth and that it is worthwhile to do so" (Stephen Neill and Tom Wright, 1998). A series of books written by him and James Duun, together with an outstandingly positive book by Richard Bauckham, *Jesus and the Eyewitnesses: The Gospels as Eyewitness Testimony* (2006), have boosted this optimism.

However, there is still huge disagreement among scholars. The Jesus Seminar in particular has become widely known for its sceptical stance. Founded in 1985 by Robert Funk, the Seminar was very active through the 1980s and 1990s, and into the early twenty-first century. Its purpose was to establish a collective view of the historicity of the deeds and sayings of Jesus. Its methodology was unusual and distinctive. It employed a voting system using coloured beads to reach its results. It discovered that 82% of the words ascribed to Jesus in the gospels were not actually spoken by him and 84% of the deeds attributed to Jesus in the gospels were not authentic.

The work of the Jesus Seminar was met by a storm of criticism from other scholars. On what grounds? Many have commented on their presuppositions, considering that the Seminar operates to a remarkable degree on a priori principles, some of them reflecting anti-supernatural bias. Secularist scholars may ask, however, what is the matter with that? Is it not only the opposite of the religious bias that motivates so many other scholars?

At this point it may be helpful to put the difficulties experienced by scholars into a wider context. Their work must be seen against the background which the Questers inherited. The Enlightenment stress on the role of reason in deciding on truth-questions was in strong reaction to what appeared to be the traditional Christian attitude towards the Bible.

Reaction against traditional Christian approaches to the gospels

The traditional approach by Christians, whether of the Orthodox, Catholic or Protestant churches, tended to take the truth of everything in the gospels for granted without further enquiry. They termed the Bible the Word of God; in disputes about what Christians should believe or how they should act, the phrase "the Bible says" was – and still is – used by many Christians.

A proper veneration for scripture as handing down tradition has for many been seen as veneration for the actual literal meaning of the text of scripture, as though scripture can never err. (See my book *Truth and Scripture* (2004), Chapter 8.) The term fundamentalist is commonly used to describe this attitude, but in a less articulated way it still runs like a thread through how many Christians view the Bible. Important work by R.C.T. and A.T. Hanson on the Early Fathers shows that this approach has a long history: "Their reverence for the biblical text misled them. They could not admit seriously that the books were the product of human minds. The result was a great deal of wondrous and even learned nonsense" (1989, p.34, p. 122).

It has meant that traditionally there has been little proper historical enquiry into who Jesus was as a human person and what he actually taught, and how he related to first-century

Palestine. Taking the gospels on trust, it was easily assumed that there could be no mistakes or misunderstandings conveyed by scripture. To approach the gospels in a spirit of critical enquiry appeared to undermine the proper attitude of receptivity and obedience to the message of the Bible. Questions, except purely for elucidation, were regarded as inappropriate. Strictly textual criticism and much intelligent concern regarding translation was encouraged and achieved a high standard of scholarship. Interpretation of the content of the text, however, received much less critical attention, and attention to the actual character of Jesus, as a person living at a precise time and place, even less. As James Dunn and Scot McKnight put it in their book *The Historical Jesus in Recent Research*: "For most Christians, for most of Christianity's history, there was something offensive, even blasphemous, in asking how this Jesus might have lived, even in envisaging him eating ordinary food, or laughing and joking with his friends, or in burping or being sick" (2005, p. xi).

Instead, the four gospels tended to be used largely as resources for worship and devotion. Discrete passages read out in church services, and encouragement to find inspiration for private devotion, meant that the gospels were largely seen in this light and not as historical source material. This was aided and abetted since the sixteenth century by the Reformation split with Catholicism. The gospels, along with the rest of the Bible, became a weapon in the fractious debate over what constitutes authentic authority for Christians. Should Christians trust the Church, particularly the Papacy, or does final authority lie *sola scriptura*: solely in the Bible?

The relationship of the gospels to history has been brought vividly to light during the quests. The anti-historical strand in traditional Christian approaches to the gospels was indeed inadequate, and not only on historical grounds. Theologically too, for the stated faith of Christians in Jesus as God and man necessarily entails regarding history as crucially important. To believe that God thought it worthwhile to take upon himself the incredibly complex purpose of being incarnated as a real human being demands that history be taken seriously. For it confers on the status of the world and of humanity something so worthwhile that it cannot be just denigrated to a postscript and failed to be taken seriously.

The relationship of history to what is termed the supernatural

Today some, however, would argue that a historian has indeed to be anti-supernatural to do history at all. The proper study of the past began when events were no longer seen as possibly ascribed to the gods but perceived in empirical terms. To allow for the possibility of other agency in history would be a retrograde step permitting superstition and magic again to hold sway.

This is where there is a particular problem regarding religious texts. Belief in God, and in the possibility of Spiritual/ Transcendent Reality relating in specific ways to the natural world, is not something which can be empirically proved. This presents a particular difficulty for people who see history as a purely empirical study which is how it tends to be viewed today by so many. They have to make an assumption which cannot be verified by historical research, and which is therefore ideological. For those who assume the non-existence of any Transcendent element in the reality of the world necessarily have to discount any reference to the divine in a text.

The assumption of a religious belief is not, however, so constrained. It does not automatically close down historical enquiry. Instead, because it has not already excluded the possibility of any divine intervention, it is free to explore the evidence claimed for particular incidents. It is not obliged to accept that a miracle occurred, but it can be open to enquiry as to whether it occurred in a particular instance. It has not dogmatically decided beforehand that no miracle could have happened.

So it happens that, if the traditional understanding of the gospels was unnecessarily dogmatic, the sceptical reaction to this is equally dogmatic and this time necessarily so, in failing to take historical enquiry seriously enough. In place of "Gospel truth", ironically, trust could now be placed in "Gospel untruth"!

Why does history have to be seen as only taking account of empirical evidence?

If history is the search for what actually happened, as Ranke who is regarded as the founder of the modern discipline of history put it, and as will be discussed in the next chapter, then if something beyond the everyday empirically understandable world of experience happened the historian, as historian, is in no position to say that it did not happen. After all, if what happened did happen, then it is the historian who needs to adjust her/his preconceptions to fit the evidence; it should not be the other way round: the evidence being made to fit the theory. Rather, it is the historian's job to examine all the historical evidence available to try to reach as fair an opinion concerning it as possible. For if something happened it cannot be deemed on critical grounds not to have happened just because a historian did not expect it to happen.

History does not need to be seen as purely empirical study. Ranke himself did not see history in that light. As a teacher of Classics, he became interested in history in part because of his desire to be involved in the developing field of a more professionalised history, and in part because of his desire to find the hand of God in the workings of history (Boldt, 2016), In a series of lectures given before the future King Maximilian II of Bavaria in 1854, Ranke argued that the historian must seek the "Holy hieroglyph" in history. He considered that "every age is next to God": God gazes over history in its totality and finds all periods equal. For Ranke history was more than empirical study.

That it became narrowed down is a result of the hold of positivism or scientism amongst the academic elite during the nineteenth and twentieth centuries. A scientific approach to knowledge was so highly valued that historians tried to follow suit making their subject as close to a science as possible. (See discussion of this in Chapter 3.) Equating what is historical with what is just empirical is, as it were, an accident of the Enlightenment. In fact, it has resulted in emphasizing an aspect of Enlightenment thought which has unknowingly become a major characteristic of the West.

Scholars pursuing the quest, generally, insist that they do so on historical grounds. Yet all depends on how history is understood. Thus, it comes about that appeal to history per se by the Questers may be useless, because the understanding of history has already been narrowed down to exclude enquiry into the possibility of the spiritual; it has to assume its non-existence in the gospels. In the process, certain foundational historical principles have often been forgotten or ignored.

I argue that the quest for the historical Jesus has still not been a conspicuous success. This is because it has often not been conducted along properly historical lines, despite that being the avowed intention. What is needed is a much deeper awareness of what history properly involves, in particular the basic principles which such study should respect. If such historical principles are at work, I consider that we can reach considerable reliability concerning the historical Jesus. To that I now turn in the next chapter.

Chapter 3

The Nature of History

Seeking to understand Jesus as a human person is necessarily a historical study. This chapter therefore looks at what History involves. It does need to be distinguished from other modes of enquiry and thinking which have their distinctive dominant focal points. Thus, Geography is concerned with place, the Sciences with aspects of the physical world, Sociology with how people relate to each other in communities, Arts subjects with how aesthetic creativity is expressed, etc.

It is necessary, however, to bear in mind that these subject divisions do not exist in the real world. They are convenient tools for thinking about that world which has to be understood holistically, aided by attention to particular aspects of it.

Understanding of Jesus of Nazareth will always transcend any of the categories our minds use to find out about him. Meier, a distinguished contemporary Quester, has a fascinating comment on this. "In contrast to the 'real Jesus', the 'historical Jesus' is that Jesus whom we can recover or reconstruct by using the scientific tools of modern historical research. The 'historical Jesus' is thus a scientific construct, a theoretical abstraction of modern scholars that coincides only partially with the real Jesus of Nazareth, the Jew who actually lived and worked in Palestine in the first century AD" (1991, p. 4).

I see this comment as partly true and partly not! The human mind will never be able to appreciate the real Jesus of Nazareth, even though study can enable us to get closer to him as a person than would otherwise be possible. The statement is, however, deeply mistaken in another way. It implies the operation of Lessing's ditch which was mentioned in Chapter 2. It creates a false dichotomy between study and what is to be studied.

Whether study is helpful in reaching understanding of its subject matter depends on the quality of the study: on such factors as focussed attention, hard work, a proper spirit of openness to what is being discovered, and integrity shielding against irrelevant agendas. A further criticism of Meier's comment will be discussed below under the section on whether history can be called a science.

The practice of history

History concerns the human past in events, people, circumstances, and ways of thinking and behaving. As such, people have been interested in and studying history since time immemorial. It is of perennial interest. As a professional subject studied in universities, History goes back to the early nineteenth century. Leopold von Ranke (1795–1886) is regarded as "the father as well as the master of modern historical scholarship" (Stern (ed.), 1973, p. 54). His method of teaching at the University of Berlin through seminars became widely copied. He developed a structure and methodology for the subject which included especially an emphasis on genuine and original documents, on primary sources by comparison with secondary sources, on the value of narratives of eyewitnesses and so forth. These all need to be examined from the point of view of such questions as chronology, context and causation.

Chronology is crucial. In archaeology enormous care must be taken regarding the strata in which finds appear. The dating of them places them in a particular era. The same is true of texts. Anachronisms occur when this principle is ignored. A famous example is that found in Shakespeare's play *Julius Caesar*. In Act 2, Scene 1 Cassius tells the other conspirators that the clock struck three. Since clocks that could move and "strike" had not yet been invented in classical times, this may indicate Shakespeare's sense of humour depending on its factually being out of place.

Consideration of context is vital. What people do and say always belongs to their time. Dress is one of the clearest examples of the specificity of situations. A Roman senator did not dress like a sixteenth-century English merchant. The characteristics of the time when events happened is crucial for interpretation. The current vogue for virtue signalling concerning, for example, slavery is guilty of ignoring the prevailing tendencies and possibilities open to people who lived in the past. Thus, to topple the statue of a slave trader such as Edward Colston of Bristol because of his failing to abide by modern standards of outlook on slavery shows deep misunderstanding of the nature of history.

Historians have to be much concerned about causality. It is no easy matter to establish the cause of events, and not simply a coincidence that certain facts seemed to precede others. The fact that there was a bad harvest and danger of starvation for some people prior to the French Revolution does not necessarily supply a cause for it. It may have had little or nothing to do with it but perhaps have been exploited even at the time by those truly responsible for the Revolution. Marie Antoinette's famous comment concerning starving peasants, "If they cannot eat bread, let them have cake", was attributed to her years after her execution. The causes of the French Revolution were almost certainly many, and clear evidence is needed to establish that the luxury of Marie Antoinette in particular had much to do with it. That the revolutionary fervour of the radical reformers was a potent cause can be established on historical grounds. It was intellectuals who led the Revolution, not peasants or working folk, and those intellectuals had been listening for a long time to the thoughts of radical reformers such as Diderot. The inspiration of the American War of Independence is also strongly suggested by the involvement of Thomas Paine. (See, e.g., *Thomas Paine and the French Revolution*, Carine Lounissi, 2018.)

Facts and interpretation

Many people have memories of being taught history as a series of facts. Yet what historians have to try to do is establish what the facts are. To assume that facts are straightforward and just to be learnt is seriously mistaken. As a result of hard work by historians, certain pieces of information can come accurately to reflect what happened, for example, that in 1066 William the Conqueror won the Battle of Hastings which led to the dismantling of the Anglo-Saxon kingdom. The meaning and impact of this fact, however, depends on a whole series of other enquiries, and there is no guarantee that the interpretation is correct.

Data by itself does not make history; it is inert, just separate things, unless embedded in a meaningful narrative. Interpretation is crucial. Just because a few pottery shards originating in the eastern Mediterranean have been found in a ship further west is not necessarily evidence of trading; a traveller could have carried a container with him, having picked it up who knows where. Finds of Roman coins being used to date, say, a grave are not by themselves conclusive; certainly a coin of Hadrian may indicate the earliest that a grave was used, but it could have been much later. So many factors need to be taken into account as to the significance of data, and this is what historians try to do.

Interpretation is therefore vital in history, and this always extends well beyond so-called facts. Because interpretation necessarily involves the subjectivity of the historian, history can never deliver absolute certainty; enquiry must always be ongoing. We can never be really sure that X said precisely this, or that Y did that, or that Z was caused by this and not that. Understanding in history is always partial and provisional.

The desire for certainty, however, runs deep and appears irresistible. It needs constantly to be guarded against. Lucy Worsley, in her interesting TV programmes on Fibs in American and in British history, clearly expressed the way in which we easily accept that history is fixed and straightforward when "it's not like that at all". Instead, there are many voices talking about the past, and the loudest tend to predominate. What has thus been taken on board by most people may turn out to be mistaken, as further investigation can show. Her programmes give many examples.

It is important, however, not to rush to the opposite conclusion and consider that all we have in History is a cacophony of voices in which virtually anything goes. We can all say what we like, because there are just as many histories as there are people to think them up. This reaction needs to be guarded against because of the impact of postmodernism which has questioned the very notion of truth. In recent debate over the woke agenda phrases such as my truth or your truth have been in vogue. With its talk of history being about diverse stories, it has tended to leave the impression that we can know nothing reliably in history at all. This is false in the opposite direction. We can know a great deal if careful historical principles are followed. The results are nearer or further from the truth according to the skill and experience and integrity of the historian who is doing the investigation.

To do this, historical enquiry will sometimes resemble scientific investigation and techniques in order to assemble essential data. What therefore is the relationship between the sciences and history?

Is History a science? The case against similarity

History can never literally be a science because the differences are significant. Firstly, the sheer uniqueness of what happened in the past makes history a very different subject from science. Whilst scientists can set up experiments which can be to some extent objectively assessed, what happened in history cannot be experimented with in that way. History concerns unique instances and is not repeatable. Science looks for general laws, for what is universal and happens all the time. History, on the other hand, has to beware of generalizations. It is unrepeatable and dependent on the chance evidence left behind.

Secondly, the basic unit to be explored in history is human behaviour which can never be set out in inflexible and therefore absolutely certain principles. Assessing how and why human beings act necessarily involves subjective appreciation. It calls for a very special kind of approach by the investigator which constitutes a major difference between science and history.

A deep commitment to the search for truth, and an awareness of a sense of wonder play a huge part in motivating the scientist, but for the historian there is more to be said. To discover that water = H2O does not of itself require a particularly constructive mindset. To get on the wavelength of an Oliver Cromwell or a Charles I is, however, essential for any properly historical understanding of the English Civil War of the seventeenth century. The question is: how is this to be reached?

Wright has something very important to say on this. He speaks of "an epistemology of love" as necessary. By love he means "exercising sympathetic imagination whether called love or not" (2019, p. 103). The basic dilemma facing the historian is that people are unique and therefore have to be understood individually. This means that we have "to attend to the aims and motives of people different from ourselves" (2019, p. 98). This is far from easy.

The current anxiety over the importance of accepting the principle of diversity in public life precisely reflects the challenge that this presents. We all tend to be comfortable with the known and afraid of the unfamiliar. Indeed, for safety's sake we may all be hardwired to be like this. To overcome this inner barrier, we need powerful emotional as well as cognitive motivation. This is why Wright uses the word love even though, as a term, it has been heavily abused in the modern world.

He issues a warning. "The sympathetic imagination required

for the formation of hypotheses must never mean that we imagine people in other cultures and ages to be just like ourselves." He goes on to quote J.G. Hamann: "Each has its own vocabulary which can be grasped only with the passion of a friend, an intimate, a lover." Wright depicts a lover as "one who simultaneously enters sympathetically into the life of the beloved while honoring and celebrating the vital differences between the two of them" (2019, p. 97). Again, he notes: "When I love I am delightedly engaged with that which is other than myself. Part of the delight is precisely in allowing it – or him, or her – to be the 'other', to be different" (2019, p. 103). Applying this approach results in not "mere random guesswork but in the kind of knowledge on which real people do stake their real lives" (2019, p. 102).

Is History a science? The case for similarity

There are, however, important similarities between History and the sciences. As Wright puts it: History is "a close cousin of the hard sciences" (2019, p. 101). In science, a rigorous discipline pursues the question of truth, and it must do so in history. The distinction between a historical novel and history per se must always be kept in mind. In the first the writer utilises historical data to compile a story in the artistic sense of the word. In the latter the historian seeks to have everything written supported by evidence. So, in this crucial respect history is like science; it should receive the same kind of respect from other scholars.

History is also similar to science in another aspect. The notion that science delivers absolute reliability is false. It sets up hypotheses and judges them to the best of the ability of scientists, but the status of scientific pronouncements is, like in History, partial and provisional. Science is always ongoing work; hypotheses stand until they are falsified; fresh evidence has to be taken seriously. History therefore is not unique in delivering a certainty which is but partial and provisional.

It is important, however, not to over stress the closeness

of the relationship. Many scholars have done this. Such is the pull of science for making academic work appear scholarly that many people do speak of History as a science, admittedly a social science, nevertheless they use this word. History has been presented as a quasi-science, along the lines of Comte's social science project. Ranke, for example, has often been seen as "the pioneer of a critical historical science" (e.g., Breisach, 2007, p. 233).

In a detailed discussion on a university exam paper at Utkal University in Odisha, India, for History, the case against considering history to be a science is strongly expressed, yet the writers are still reluctant not to call History a science as well:

"History is a science in the sense that it pursues its own techniques to establish and interpret facts. Like other natural sciences such as Physics and Chemistry it uses various methods of enquiry such as observation, classification, experiment and formulation of hypothesis and analysis of evidence before interpreting and reconstructing the past. History also follows the scientific method of enquiry to find out the truth" (Pallavi Talekau, Dr. Jyotrimayee Nayak, Dr.S. Harichandan, p. 5).

Many techniques for studying data are indeed shared between science and History. The last sentence in the quotation above gives, however, cause for alarm, for it implies that in order to find truth scientific principles must be utilised. This is close to the approach of scientism which denies the validity of other ways towards knowledge. It encapsulates the Positivist streak which is still powerfully at work in academe generally.

This attitude has profoundly affected how many scholars approach the quest for the historical Jesus. They tend to follow Meier's definition given above. His comment clearly reveals the discrepancy between scholarly study and real historical search for understanding. It is Lessing's ditch in practice; it implies scholars constructing their views of Jesus on one side, and believers in a real Jesus on the other.

The problem leading to this either/or approach is over-concern with presumed objectivity which has tended to take over in universities generally. It is crucial to distinguish between positivism and the straightforward concern of historians like Ranke who saw history as concerned with *wie es eigentlich gewesen*: "how things actually were". The modern study of history has had from the first to be on guard against takeover by non-historical theories and views. The notion of progress was a favourite theme of the nineteenth century promoted by many philosophers such as Hegel and taken up by Marx. This is very much what Ranke was up against. He was reacting against over-blown idealist conceptions of the purpose and ongoing nature of history. Ranke was not interested in using history as a driver for metaphysical notions.

Knowledge in history, as for almost all walks of life apart from strict science, is unavoidably linked to experience which is personal, subjective to a degree and impossible therefore to be adequately ratified by so-called objective criteria. Where scientifically collected data is available and relevant, historians will use it, but not otherwise. The historian Lynn Hunt summarises it: "Despite its occasional reliance on scientific techniques, History is not a science. It is a literary art that uses scientific techniques where relevant but whose fundamental aim is to tell a true story" (2018).

The emphasis here is on the search for truth. Use of the word "story" can be questioned for its usefulness because it easily conjures up the notion of people just making up things as they wish. This is why the closeness of history with science does need asserting as much as the differences. The search for historical data requires a discipline not dissimilar to that of scientists. As Wright points out: "There is a continuum, rather than a great gulf, between 'science' and 'history'....We know that the Romans destroyed Jerusalem in AD 70 just as surely as we know that 'water' equals 'hydrogen plus oxygen'" (2019, p. 100).

Concern for evidence: an example

The obligation to search for truth remains central to the historian's task. It means that evidence is needed to support what is said. To take a highly controversial subject of enquiry, the resurrection of Jesus, it is instructive to consider the status of the arguments used to support the historical understanding of it.

Historians cannot get round the fact that Christianity arose at a specific time around the belief that the crucified Jesus had risen from the dead. The evidence of the gospels in favour of its being a real event, not just something the disciples conjured up in their own minds, will be looked at in Chapter 8. The arguments put forward by those who consider that it was not a historical event illustrate, however, what absence of historical evidence looks like, namely conjecture based on personal preferences. It offers an example of reliance on a non-historical approach.

A variety of alternative explanations for the supposed resurrection of Jesus have been put forward.

(i) Reimarus right at the beginning of the Quest offered the suggestion that the disciples of Jesus stole his body, and that this accounts for the resurrection myth and all that followed from it.

(ii) Friedrich Schleiermacher and others right up to the present day have favoured the swoon theory which suggested that Jesus survived the crucifixion. He was brought down from the cross alive and recovered.

(iii) The currently most favoured naturalistic theory to account for the resurrection is the Hallucination or Subjective Vision theory. According to this view some of the followers of Jesus experienced a trance-like vision of him in the manner of fantasists whose imagination conjures up what seems real to them but to no one else. This notion was initially popularised by Strauss, and others such as Ernest Renan followed him. The popularity of this thesis continues into the present.

(iv) Some scholars favour a more precise psychological explanation. One example is that put forward by Gerd Ludemann who considers that Peter in Galilee had a vision of Jesus which was induced by feelings of guilt for betraying Jesus. Peter experienced this as a real appearance of Jesus forgiving him and raised him from the dead. The change in him convinced the other disciples that the resurrection of Jesus was real. He gives a similar explanation for Paul also (2004).

How historically plausible are any of these theories?

(i) Where is the evidence for the disciples of Jesus stealing his body? Quite apart from the difficulty presented by assuming that so successful a movement was based on an outright lie, it fails to account for the intrepid devotion of the disciples, even up to the point of risking death itself. That it was a notion mentioned in the gospels and dismissed at the time can come as no surprise. It is an obvious possibility for those who did not wish to consider the alternative of his resurrection, but it had no evidence to support it except that the tomb was found vacant. A variation suggested that the actual burial site had been mistaken, but again there is no evidence for this.

(ii) It is hard to take the swoon theory seriously. Crucifixion was a terrible form of death, and the likelihood of anyone surviving it relatively remote. Josephus in fact records an example when a friend of his survived crucifixion through the help of a physician. That such was possible concerning

Jesus is highly unlikely. Moreover, a decrepit, traumatised Jesus would never have galvanised the disciples into their rock-like certainty that he was alive again. It is at odds with the gospel evidence. The first Christians preached not his survival, nor that the crucifixion did not kill him, but his resurrection.

(iii) There is huge uncertainty regarding the subjective vision explanation. Can it account for the communal viewings reported in the New Testament? Are its effects sufficient to establish long-term transformation of character? How could such a type of vision lead people affected by it to believe in a risen Jesus when visions always happen because someone is dead? As Wright argues, visions of the dead were always associated with spirits and ghosts, and never with bodily resurrection. Such visions meant precisely, as people in the ancient and modern worlds have discovered, that the person was dead, not that they were alive.

(iv) Accounting for belief in the resurrection on psychological grounds may appear to be a strong option, so I will consider it in a little more detail. Basically, there is insufficient data to do a psychoanalysis of Peter; the information about Peter's psyche is, by Lüdemann's own admission, "incomparably worse" than it is for Paul. His whole theory is based on imaginative conjecture about Peter's psychological state, of which we know almost nothing.

Psychoanalysis is notoriously difficult even with a patient seated on the couch in front of the analyst, but it is virtually impossible with historical figures. The historian is concerned with how and why human beings act and therefore considers psychological factors in seeking to interpret the past, but such musings cannot pretend to have a scientific status. The German historian of religion Martin Hengel rightly concludes, "Lüdemann ... does not recognise these limits on the historian. Here he gets into the realm of psychological explanations, for which no verification is really possible ... the sources are far too limited for such psychologising analyses" (1991, p. 79).

The sheer abundance of theories put forward, together with the fact that none of these can claim the universal assent of other sceptical scholars, argues against any of them. Nor are any of them supported by historical evidence.

The importance of history

To conclude this chapter, history with its concern for the past also aids understanding of the present and thinking towards the future. Indeed, the point can be made the other way round. Those who fail to understand the past may well be doomed to repeat it. The well-being of the future depends on coming to terms with the past.

To take but one example. There are lessons to be learnt from assuming that change can be forced on people, as all revolutionaries as well as politically correct movements so easily believe; it cannot be. Were this insight to be taken on board, it would help to prevent some of the terrible errors of the past when in seeking to end one kind of injustice, other injustice results. Historians know well that very often the result of revolutions is not real change but simply different people in power, as Orwell so brilliantly satirised in his writing in *Animal Farm*.

Political activists of all persuasions should take note. Angry movements, however morally justified, which accuse other people of racism, for example, only reinforce what is wrong with racism, namely that the colour of a person's skin actually matters. The lesson to be learnt for civilisation is that everyone matters regardless of the colour of their skin: that is what needs nurturing.

Moreover, there is an even deeper point to be made. Past

injustice cannot be put right by a spirit of vindictiveness and blame, but only by forgiveness and reconciliation. The example of Mandela and Desmond Tutu at the ending of Apartheid in South Africa showed the world the creative power of such an approach, just as vindictiveness towards Germany after WWI helped to lay the seed for WWII. These are very hard lessons for human beings to learn, but a knowledge of history can help to teach them.

Finally, instead of seeing the necessarily subjective aspect of history as a disadvantage, we ought to appreciate the vastly more comprehensive and fascinating quest for knowledge and understanding which History represents. Nevertheless, historians do have to guard against pure subjectivity. There are indeed certain historical principles which should be adhered to if the results are to be accorded the status of responsible History. The next chapter will discuss the first of these.

Chapter 4

Giving Initial Benefit of Doubt: 1st Historical Principle

Proponents of reason have been trusting its validity to discount religious faith. Does this provide a sound rational basis for challenging the gospels? I maintain that it does not because it ignores three foundational historical principles. The first of these is the need to give initial benefit of doubt to historical material. This will form the subject of this and the next chapter.

The first historical principle concerns beginning by giving benefit of doubt to the text. The fragility of what happens to survive from the past gives it a special, indeed precious, value. The historian must have respect for the surviving data unless there are historical reasons for challenging it. The source, as one of the bits and pieces which happen to have survived the vicissitudes of time, has a status that doubts cannot have. The distinguished Anglo-Saxon historian James Campbell liked to recall "that of an estimated 18 million discharge certificates given to soldiers of the Roman empire, only seven had been found" (Obituary, *The Times*, 8 July 2016).

A source should only be set aside for sound and strong reasons. Lynn Hunt gives a clear example of failure to observe giving such initial benefit of the doubt. "When Obama presented his birth certificate, confirming that he had been born in the state of Hawaii, Trump immediately retorted that it might be fraudulent, even though he had no evidence that it was falsified" (2018, p. 2).

Nevertheless, in the realm of biblical scholarship and the quest for the historical Jesus, this principle of giving initial benefit of the doubt is likely to be challenged by many. Indeed, the Jesus Seminar included as one of their major principles withholding benefit of doubt from the gospels. See discussion in Chapter 2. It is worth therefore to consider in some detail just why giving initial benefit of the doubt to source material is so essential: why it is a fundamental principle not to be set aside. There are at least four considerations.

(i) The primacy of trust: were fraudulence to be the norm...

If Trump's approach, given above, to the evidence for Obama's birth were applied to everything, the whole of civilisation would grind to a standstill. In normal life we all have to operate basically on trust, not the other way round. It is foundational; without it civilised life is not possible. We couldn't drive a car on the road without trust, even though we know that accidents can happen.

In conversation with people, to assume that everything they say is unreliable will soon end the possibility of any personal encounter. We just have to trust people initially even though we know they may not be wholly trustworthy regarding anything they say. We have to give them benefit of the doubt unless something occurs to make us question that.

Such trust is especially needed in situations of confrontation where there is much disagreement in opinion. A meeting of minds and hearts has to be based on initial trust which takes the other person seriously as a person, is prepared to listen properly to what s/he speaks from their own experience and therefore enables real debate on what it is that divides them. To treat an opponent with suspicion and hostility is to ensure breakdown in relationship and ever renewed misunderstanding.

Unless some initial trust is mutually shown, what, for example, can help to heal the deep rift between Democrats and Republicans in the USA which has recently so gravely threatened the practice of democracy? Ronald Dworkin, the American philosopher and political jurist, in a book significantly titled *Is Democracy Possible Here?*, gave a devastating prophecy of the weakness of democratic dialogue in America: "We are no longer partners in self-government; our politics are rather a form of war." He nevertheless saw a realistic way forward for a liberal democracy because he considers that both sides in the American divide do share fundamental values. "It would be silly to expect that Americans will cease to disagree radically about politics any time soon. It would nevertheless be a great improvement if they came to see their continuing controversies as about the best interpretation of fundamental values they all share rather than simply as confrontations between two divergent world-views neither of which is comprehensible to the other" (2006, p. 1, p. 22).

Primacy of trust applied to a historical text

In all thinking, positive assumptions have to be made to get going at all. It is the same for the historian; initial trust for the source is unavoidable. There has to be a starting point. If it is genuine enquiry and the original was a mistake or fraudulent, this is likely to emerge. That is why initial benefit of doubt should be given.

To regard the diary of Samuel Pepys, for example, as suspect from the start, namely, that every entry could be mistaken wilfully or not, would render its valuable historical source material useless. Enquiry would always be in the form of "supposing that this happens to be true when it may not be." This would make the historian's job impossible. Why should we doubt his comment about scorched pigeons falling from the skies during the Great Fire of London?

As his biographer, Claire Tomalin, notes, in coming to understand such events as the Great Plague of London and the Great Fire, he "was more significant than may appear at first glance, because the censorship imposed by the government of

Charles II ensured that there were no newspapers at this period except for a single government-controlled information sheet, the London Gazette. It meant that no proper record of public events was being kept, and even parliamentary debates were not allowed to be reported."

Even more can be said. If what was written in *The London Gazette* is subject to the initial assumption that none of it may be true, there would be no means whatever of proceeding with any enquiry.

The important word is *initial* giving benefit of the doubt. Giving such respect to the evidence does not mean that the elaborate edifice of learned enquiry is misplaced. Rigorous enquiry is indeed needed. What it does mean is that a rational approach will not start with criticism but with presumption of honest intention. Immediately to doubt the veracity of a source is a negative reaction which does not accord such respect. Even if the text turns out to be, after enquiry, guilty of various faults, these should not be presumed at the beginning. Historical evidence is needed to show up mistakes, misunderstandings, faulty memory, sheer ignorance, over-highlighting what is not especially important, masking out what may be important, as well as deliberate fraud.

Initial benefit of doubt should therefore be accorded to it unless there are good reasons for not doing so. Are there any such good reasons for initial suspicion?

(i) An obvious case is if the source proclaims itself to be fantasy and therefore not history; historical novels fall into this category. The only requirement regarding being truthful is to remind readers that the material should not be given benefit of the doubt by mistake or through ignorance.

(ii) If there is sound and strong historical reasoning why a source should be regarded with suspicion, then it should not receive benefit of the doubt. Indeed, this is so, but how has the presumed historical reasoning emerged? Presumably only by doing research and based on what – on initial suspicion of the source material? In which case what is being trusted, and why?

It is worth considering here an impediment which has been much encouraged in the West:

Over-stressing the need for critical thinking

Since the Enlightenment the West as a whole has tended to imply that thinking involves necessarily criticism; there has not been a similar stress on affirmation. Indeed, the reverse is more generally the case; tradition of any kind tends to be seen in a suspicious light. To be critical is regarded as a compliment; to adhere to tradition tends to be seen as questionable.

The over-emphasis in the West on being sceptical concerning tradition without equal emphasis on the importance first of understanding and respecting what is being criticized has been deeply misleading. It creates an unfavourable situation in conversation or debate. To appreciate what it is like to be another person, and take on board what experiences and difficulties help to account for a person's views, people must feel free to express themselves honestly in a spirit of desired collaboration. Without that, most so-called debate is phoney.

I argue elsewhere for *critical affirmation* whereby, by accepting conviction sympathetically to begin with, there is the best chance of understanding instead of misunderstanding it; this is because what is to be criticized has a chance first to be itself. A huge amount of criticism tends to be of the kind which theologian Paul Tillich once described as attacking what is not being defended! It is not infrequent, for example, in discussion of climate change to accuse an opponent of not accepting the reality of climate change when in fact they do accept it. The point at issue is what is causing the climate change. This is precisely the matter that ought to be debated but which normally is sidetracked completely.

Criticism to be of value must be based on as correct an interpretation as possible. In the case of a historical text, it can then shed light on the historical investigation as a whole. The damage done by academics insisting on the importance of being critical and sceptical without equally, or even more, emphasizing the normality of credibility has been huge. Through their great influence on society, this view has been fed through to the general public. Tarif Khalidi quotes an interesting Muslim saying: "Jesus was asked: 'Spirit and Word of God, who is the most seditious of men?' He replied: 'The scholar who is in error. If a scholar errs, a host of people will fall into error because of him'" (2020, p. 130).

The constant requirement to be critical has easily buried the need to affirm as the only basis on which criticism can take place anyway. Criticism after all is a parasite; there has to be something to criticize. To give precedence to criticism without acknowledging first its debt to what has been affirmed is dangerously one-sided. That said, the important word regarding giving historical source material the benefit of the doubt is the word initial.

(ii) The unavoidability of trusting something

Distrusting everything all the time is impossible. All historical enquiry, like all other enquiry, would collapse by the weight of this manifestly unworkable assumption. For on what basis can fraud be established, and how can investigation get started without taking something for granted: without trusting something? Wittgenstein made this point powerfully in his comment: "the game of doubting itself presupposes certainty" (1969, 114–115).

It is dishonest indeed to assume a sceptical stance for all evidence. In practice, what happens is that some evidence is accepted on the basis of which other evidence is declared invalid. Thus, Reimarus was trusting his own empirical/rational approach to knowledge, on the basis of which he denied the validity of anything miraculous recorded in the gospels.

To give a contemporary example, Eric Eve is assured that the writers of the gospels were: "people who understood truth not so much as strict correspondence with facts (the goal of positivist historiography) as bringing out the correct significance of events" (2016, p. 47). What Eve is trusting here is empirical understanding of psychology, namely that everyone has an agenda beyond concern for truth. Closely associated with it is the assumption that all religious people are out to convert, an assumption encouraged by doubt that any religious belief is true. It is, in fact, the secular agenda which regards religion as irrelevant because it cannot be proved empirically to be true.

It may be the case that religious people do have agendas, but is that not so for anyone who speaks or writes? The notion that only religious people have agendas has little rational evidence to support it; secularists have agendas too.

In Eve's comment, a great deal is built on the mindset of the early Christians so as to challenge what they put in the gospels. The evidence, however, for that mindset has to be trusted as sound in order to question what is said in the gospels. Moreover, what Eve appears to be trusting is the same as Reimarus: the positivist understanding of truth which is itself highly contentious.

(iii) The danger of any agenda taking over is great unless initial trust is given to the source material

Historians need to try to be impartial in their study and not allow their world views to interfere. A major consideration for such respect for the document is that otherwise ideology can easily creep in. A very clear example is how the assumption of a great divide between reason and faith, understood as a divide between properly intellectual enquiry and religion, such as was given vivid form in the metaphor of Lessing's ditch, has powered enquiry. The result was clearly expressed by Meier in the quotation given in Chapter 3 with its implication that study about religion is necessarily applying scientific modes of enquiry.

Not giving initial benefit of doubt to source material offers a field day for personal world views to be in the driving seat. A common reason for doubting a historical source is in fact ideological, as in the above example concerning Trump. Lack of respect for the evidence is shown every time that evidence is just put to one side if it does not happen to fit the agenda of the historian. Secret motivation below the radar can prompt scholars effectively to say: "I accept this as genuine because I want to"; or "I won't accept this as genuine because I don't want to." Yet we all know that truth does not depend on our personal wishes and assumptions. The point of enquiry and of all scholarship worthy of the name is to try to find out the truth irrespective of my or your preferences. Unrestrained by respect for the source material, scholars can feel free to fudge it according to their pre-conceived ideas.

History is not supposed to be about finding support for one's own pre-conceived world view, but it can easily lapse into becoming that without generous and honest respect for the text. Thus, Reimarus felt able to discredit the gospels for their supernatural content because he believed all that was phoney. His actual faith was in the capacity of detached reason to dismiss the gospels; he did not dismiss them because of any historical evidence he discovered.

This is where the mindset of the times can have a baleful and displacing effect. It can simply be taken as a given. We in the West are quick to see this happening in cultures centred on theological certainty of any kind, for example, the Taliban, where the will of Allah is taken for granted as known. Yet this is also precisely what has happened in the West regarding the notion of the non-existence of God as it has affected intellectuals since the Enlightenment. This mindset could be mistaken.

I hasten to respond to a possible objection. Some may be inclined to challenge this representation of the Enlightenment mind. Ritchie Robertson's recent book considers that the enmity between religion and science belonged to a later period, "For this era, scientific knowledge was the enemy of superstition, but not of religion" (*The Enlightenment: The Pursuit of Happiness 1680–1790*, enthusiastically reviewed by Tom Hunter, *The Times*, Dec 19, 2020). This is a book seeking to put the record straight concerning woke detractors of the Enlightenment for which "dead white men in periwigs" were responsible. Robertson acknowledges that religion and science can work together, for which there is abundant evidence. Yet his statement may also convey a false impression. Deists may have believed in God but they viewed all religion which claimed any revelation as superstition. See the discussion on Epicureanism in the Appendix.

(iv) Tipping the scales against the evidence which has survived

Failure to give initial benefit of the doubt represents gross unfairness to the source and a presumption of a "guilty" verdict on its reliability. It is not rational to argue that every statement made should be replete with reasons why it is not false; it would be quite impossible. If initial benefit of doubt is not given to the text that has survived, this effectively puts it into the dock as a defendant in which its validity can only be established by presumed objective evidence which has survived. This will necessarily involve promoting a verdict of guilty because what evidence survives the vicissitudes of time is largely due to chance. To want absolutely reliable evidence for the truth of what is said in the gospels to have survived is like expecting to find a needle in a haystack. It is weighting things heavily against the possibility of such certain evidence having survived, given the enormous vicissitudes over centuries.

Moreover, historians need to account for how and why the mistaken source material appeared. The evidence to demolish what a historical source says needs to be stronger than the initial presumption of accuracy. Critics should have historical evidence showing the fabrication as real, answering such questions as – who made this up? why did they? and when? It is the critic, not the source material, which initially should be put in the dock.

A comment on giving initial benefit of doubt to reports of miracles

In an intellectually largely secular age, does not any reference in the source material to the impact of what may transcend molecular reality constitute a proper reason for suspicion? The mindset of the times is indeed a given. Raymond Van Dam has argued that the current mindset on the West sees miracles by definition as defying the natural order of events, they "seem to challenge a genuine historical analysis" (1992, p. 84).

The problem here, however, is that one faith position is being substituted for another. There is no scientific evidence that such transcendence does not exist; this is an article of faith; it is what some people believe. It could be that they are mistaken for they cannot prove they are not. If such transcendence does exist, then the sceptics' initial suspicions of a text that speaks of transcendent agency is at fault.

Pursuit of the quest for the historical Jesus has often suffered from this fault right from the beginning. Chapter 2 pointed out that Reimarus presumed he could drive a coach and horses through most of the gospels on the grounds that they wrote about miracles. Raphael Lataster writes: "Sound historical methodology is necessarily dismissive of supernatural claims." This comment is referred to nine times as a key point in his article demolishing the thinking of the biblical scholar William Lane Craig (2015, pp. 59 ff).

Because denial of miracle has been a key principle for many in their attitude to the gospels, it may be helpful to conclude this chapter with further thoughts on this. If the source states anything which goes against obvious empirical/scientifically analysable knowledge, then it must be presumed false.

Today people are likely to look upon reports of healings at medieval shrines as examples of pre-scientific piety. Two points, however, need to be made:

(i) Historical reasons need to be given to discount statements concerning healing. When in 971, the remains of Saint Swithun were translated into the Old Minster at Winchester, the monastic chronicler Lantfred was an eyewitness to healings he saw performed: eight people were cured at Swithun's tomb in the fortnight before the translation ceremony on July 15, 971, and four or five were cured in the three days after the ceremony. For the next five months there was "rarely a day when no pilgrims arrived at Swithun's tomb: sometimes there were sixteen or eighteen, occasionally only three or five, but more often seven to fifteen pilgrims a day" (Translatio et Miracvla S Swithvni, See Lapidge, 2003). There is no historical reason for doubting these figures which appear modest. The undoubted reputation of St Swithun in later centuries has to have a reason for it, so this appears to be justified.

(ii) The question of how they were healed involves interpretation. Theists may consider that there was divine activity at work whilst atheists will rule out that possibility and put their trust in empirical explanations such as the impact of a placebo effect: these pilgrims had such enthusiastic faith in the healer that this affected their physical condition. Either way, interpretation depends upon what the historian happens to believe. Which interpretation is correct cannot be established by historical research, for it is a metaphysical matter.

It is important to be clear on this. Regarding initial methodology, history is indeed an empirical subject. The battle against regarding thunder in the sky as the anger of Thor has been won, as it needed to be in order to get beyond sheer unsophisticated comment as to what was the case. Patrick Geary has written; "Historians, like anthropologists, must accept their subject's system of viewing reality" (1978, p. 4). This does apply to searching for empirical grounds for discovering the truth about the past and not assuming the possibility of supernatural intervention from outside. But it is important to note that this does not, and should not, control how an empirical event is caused and interpreted, for that depends upon what the historian brings to the text.

The methodology per se of the historian is not adequate for verifying the truth of how miracles were performed, if they were. The historian cannot therefore go on to announce that historical enquiry rules out the possibility of any divine involvement. It does that only if a world view dictates it, but that itself is not empirically provable. Belief in God, that is, in the possibility of Spiritual Transcendent Reality relating in specific ways to the natural world, is not something which can be empirically proved, but neither is the opposing materialist view of the world.

Instead of scholars exhibiting a spirit of openness and generosity towards a religious text such as the gospels, there tends to have been an initial assumption of suspicion. This has shown itself in many different ways to which I now turn in the next chapter.

Chapter 5

The Impact of Failure to Observe Initial Benefit of Doubt

Not giving benefit of doubt to the gospels has wreaked serious harm on the efforts of so many scholars pursuing the Quests for the historical Jesus. There has been awareness of the danger of this but it has not been prominent enough in criticism. Thus Gregory Boyd, a philosopher and theologian who has written many books on the quest for the historical Jesus, noted when being interviewed by Lee Strobel: "Historians usually operate with the burden of proof on the historian to prove falsity or unreliability, since people are generally not compulsive liars. Without that assumption, we'd know very little about ancient history" (In Strobel, 2016, p. 127). Boyd expressed what I have just said in the previous sentence: the point was not developed, however, but part of a critique of criteria in general. Its importance has been glossed over. This chapter will look at why this is serious.

Problems concerning the gospels

Instead of being given initial benefit of the doubt the following problems have been heaped upon the gospels, not as a result of enquiry but as requiring evidence to overcome these problems. Failure to give benefit of doubt to the gospels has put them effectively in the dock to defend themselves against the fundamental charge of non-truth. They must satisfy the prosecution concerning particular charges building up towards this, charges such as the following. It makes quite a formidable list.

(i)   Dating: The dating of the gospels is presumed to be late – thirty to sixty years after Jesus' life. Hence it is presumed that they are unreliable.

(ii)   Authorship: The gospels were written anonymously. The names were given much later. So, they are not eyewitness accounts which makes their reliability questionable.

(iii)   Discrepancies: The gospels reveal many contradictions which are regarded as showing that we cannot trust what they say.

(iv)   References to the supernatural: The gospels have large numbers of these which automatically indicates their non-historicity; they have no empirically sound evidence to support them.

(v)   Much later community documents: The gospels are presumed to reflect the concerns of the time when they were written, not the time when Jesus was around.

(vi)   Agenda-controlled: The gospels reflect an agenda of wishing to convert, so the authors cannot be trusted as being interested in truth.

(vii)   Conspiracy theory: The four gospels are regarded as being specifically chosen to endorse the official, power-based leadership of the Church in the fourth century. The discovery of many other gospels which the Church ruled out as heretical has been taken as proof of this deception.

(viii)   Orality: Long dependence on oral tradition emphasised how easy it was for the original words and deeds of Jesus to become altered with every telling of the story. The actual truth of what is thus transmitted is held to be unlikely.

The overall impression is that the gospels were not intended to be read as serious history; they are just a series of anecdotes. They are not biography in any form, ancient or modern. Critical suspicion is how they should be approached.

Response to these assumed problems

The rest of this chapter will argue that the actual assumption appealed to in each of these eight charges is logically suspect. Regardless of how these assumptions are applied, when considering the historical evidence concerning the gospels they are not as rationally watertight on general grounds as they claim to be.

(i) Dating

It is mistaken simply to assume that an eyewitness account is reliable, whereas something emanating from a great distance in time from the purported event is not. This is not a valid deduction. Here is an example personally known to me. In the late 1940s an aircraft crashed in rural New Brunswick and was witnessed by three families. The reports differed in detail and emphasis as to what had occurred during the crucial seconds before the crash. My friend's father-in-law exclaimed when he read the other two reports: "That is not how it happened."

At the same time, we should be wary of assuming that later writing is automatically doubtful. Craig Blomberg notes: "The two earliest biographies of Alexander the Great were written by Arrian and Plutarch more than 400 years after Alexander's death in 323 BC, yet historians consider them to be generally trustworthy. Yes legendary material did develop over time but it was only in the centuries after these two writers" (in Strobel, 2016, p. 34). Similarly, Peter Williams draws attention to what historians claim to know about the Emperor Tiberius, contemporary with Jesus. The three later sources of Tacitus,

Suetonius and Cassius Dio, written eighty or more years after the events they describe, are regarded as more reliable than the one source written contemporary with Tiberius, that of Velleius Paterculus. This is because he was a propagandist likely to compose flattery under the patronage of Tiberius (2018, p. 40f).

Regarding the dating of the gospels, research has not established this securely. Mark is generally held to be the first gospel written because knowledge of most of it is reflected in Matthew and Luke. This is widely accepted as a resolution of the Synoptic problem. There are still, however, scholars who disagree; there is widespread agreement only that John is later.

Blomberg gives an argument for an earlier dating which has not, on historical grounds, been challenged effectively. He notes that Acts ends with Paul under house arrest. "What happens to Paul, we don't find out from Acts, probably because the book was written before Paul was put to death. That means that Acts cannot be dated any later than AD 64, the most likely date for Paul's death. Acts is the second of a two-part work which must have been written earlier than that and since Luke incorporates parts of the Gospel of Mark even earlier suggesting c. 60 AD or even a bit earlier. Jesus was put to death in 30 or 33 AD which gives a maximum gap of 30 years" (in Strobel, 2016, p. 35).

Major reliance on the 70 CE date for the writing of Mark tends indeed to rely on the interpretation of Chapter 13 which indicates that the Temple in Jerusalem had already been destroyed, as happened in that year. Yet Jesus could have predicted the end of the Temple before it happened. This means that Mark could have been written earlier. The fact that most scholars discount such a notion is not compelling. Basil Mitchell gives an example in his book *Faith and Criticism* of how, as an undergraduate, he had an argument with his tutor in ancient history who assumed that the Delphic Oracle could not predict future events. Mitchell noted that there was some experimental evidence for precognition, but he notes that his tutor was scandalized (1994, p. 61).

Are there never instances when certain events are seen ahead of time by people sufficiently perceptive? My father predicted serious trouble from Hitler as far back as 1933. Mitchell comments: "It can make a difference to one's evaluation of historical evidence whether one believes in precognition or not. And this question is an extra-historical one which has to be decided on its scientific or philosophical merits" (p. 61). Reliance therefore on Mark Chapter 13 implying that it was written after the destruction of the Temple in 70 CE is itself questionable because dependent not on historical evidence but on subjective interpretation.

(ii) Authorship

It is often assumed that if a piece of writing is anonymous its truth is to be regarded with suspicion. Yet naming an author is no guarantee of truth. Truth depends on many factors other than on who said it. It is indeed a modern problem to substitute proper discussion of what is said in favour of personalizing who said it. Thus, for example, a sound statement on educational practice may be taken more seriously by some people if they did not know that the writer was a Head of a public school, otherwise strong prejudice against private education could close down the hearing. First-century readers who valued what cultured establishment figures had to say may have been dismissive of what a relatively poorly educated writer such as Mark wrote.

Moreover, anonymity can often aid communication of truth, as when a witness would otherwise fear reprisals for speaking out. This has been the case with whistle-blowers who face the threat of losing their jobs if their identity becomes known. In trials for rape, keeping the anonymity of a possible victim may positively aid the search for the truth.

Regarding research into the gospels, Blomberg's point is

apposite: "the authors' names are unlikely to have been made up. Mark and Luke were not even among the twelve disciples. For admittedly faked gospels, the names of well-known and exemplary figures were chosen, like Philip, Peter, Mary, and James, in order to give an aura of authenticity to the writing" (in Strobel, 2016, p. 23f).

An example of justified scepticism is the case for Matthew the disciple being the author of Matthew. The passage in Matthew 9:9–12 is remarkably close to similar passages in Mark 2:14–17 and Luke 5:27–32. It looks as though Matthew copied a passage from Mark concerning the call of the tax-collector to become a disciple, but that person's name was Levi. Had the tax-collector been Matthew the disciple and author of Matthew's gospel, he would have had no need to copy anything because he would have been speaking from his own experience. Moreover, the fact that Mark and Luke call the tax-collector by a different name, that of Levi, certainly sows doubt on the notion of Matthew as one of the twelve disciples.

(iii) Discrepancies

The notion that discrepancies show the unreliability of sources can be turned on its head. If, in trying to solve a who-done-it, diverse witnesses interviewed individually all come up with literally identical stories, collusion could well be suspected. Some discrepancies are exactly what one may predict if collusion has not taken place.

Discrepancies do indeed call for the attention of the historian, but unless one holds to the mythical notion that no one ever makes mistakes they do not per se render the text inauthentic. An example has already been given under (i) Dating.

Simon Greenleaf of Harvard Law School after studying the level of consistency among the four gospels wrote this: "There is enough of discrepancy to show that there could have been no previous concert among them; and at the same time such substantial agreement as to show that they all were independent narrators of the same great transaction" (in Strobel, 2016, p. 48). Thus the fact that the accounts of the women visiting the tomb of Jesus appear to contradict each other actually strengthens, rather than weakens, their claim to overall veracity. If such an extraordinary occurrence as the resurrection of Jesus were true, how likely is it that the first witnesses would not be so overwhelmed with the strangeness and immensity of what had happened that their memories of precise details would not become muddled?

The case can, moreover, be argued the other way round. If, as some sceptics like to claim, the whole event of the resurrection was invented to bolster the early Church, would they not have ensured that there were no discrepancies to cast doubt on their narrative?

(iv) References to the supernatural

In many ways this is the major assumption which so many scholars have held when enquiring about the historical Jesus. See above. It involves an ideological stance being imposed upon the historical study; it is not something which emerges from the evidence. If on grounds other than historical a person doubts the existence of any Transcendence, believing that everything is basically physical with no reference to any kind of spiritual reality beyond what scientists may be able eventually to understand, then there can be no openness to enquire into the relative historical evidence for some presumed miracle; such an interpretation is ruled out from the start.

This was very clearly the case for Reimarus, as it was for Paine and Carrier quoted above. Lataster in the article mentioned in Chapter 3 also quotes Thomas Paine's view that it is far more likely that a person simply lied than that "nature should go out of her course". This is ideological and not historical reasoning. If the possibility of the existence of God is accepted, then enquiry concerning the occurrence of miracle which is necessarily exceptional can take place.

Associated with the scepticism is misunderstanding indeed of the nature of miracle which is not anti-nature but the divine working within nature. The religious belief with which there is disagreement is not in some fictitious supernatural being lording it over the natural course of events, but the quiet activity of divine intention within what is natural. The fact that no one, religious or not, regards miracle as happening all the time, means, however, that claims to miracle do need to run the gauntlet of serious enquiry and not to be assumed.

It is important to note that there is no need to go to the other extreme and argue for the historical validity of all the miraculous elements recorded in the gospels; on the contrary, history is concerned with what happened but once. See the next chapter for discussion on this. Reports of miracle must be investigated one by one. What proper openness does not permit is a blanket dismissal of them all without historical enquiry.

Boyd writes: "Everyone would agree that you don't appeal to supernatural causes if you don't have to. But these scholars go beyond that and say you don't ever have to. They operate under the assumption that everything in history has happened according to their own experiences, and since they've never seen the supernatural, they assume miracles have never occurred in history." He goes on to add: "What I can't grant is the tremendous presumption that we know enough about the universe to say that God – if there is a God – can never break into our world in a supernatural way…That's not a presumption based on history; now you're doing metaphysics" (in Strobel, 2016, p. 126).

(v) Much later community documents
The impulse to write down what is remembered concerning the origins of a community does not of itself denote fraud, or the

desire to create or indulge in imaginary speculation. Unless the reminiscing concerns the remote past there is likely to be little opportunity to make things up. This is because of the presence of witnesses whose knowledge includes much of what actually happened. In any case, why should a thriving community have recourse to pretending to have imaginary roots?

For enduring mythology to develop many generations are needed; it does not happen overnight. The distance between the death of Jesus and the writing of three of the gospels, even by conservative estimates, was only 30–50 years – two generations at the most. As William Lane Craig put it: "The time span necessary for significant accrual of legend concerning the events of the gospels would place us in the second century AD, just the time in fact when the legendary apocryphal gospels were born. These are the legendary accounts sought by the critics." Strobel adds: "When Julius Muller in 1844 challenged anyone to find a single example of legend developing that fast in history, the response from the scholars of his day – and to the present time – was resounding silence" (Strobel, 2016, p. 28).

Blomberg makes a strong point concerning the absence of material in the gospels providing answers for problems and differences of opinion which arose in the Early Church. "We don't find anything in the gospels on particular issues which bothered the early church – whether believers should be circumcised, regulating speaking in tongues, keeping Jew and Gentile united, appropriate roles for women in ministry, could believers divorce non-Christian spouses" (In Strobel, 2016, p. 44).

Yet the application of this assumption to the gospels has been very widespread, indulged in by both religious and nonreligious scholars. Bultmann, for example, as Wright put it: "saw the four gospels as primarily witnesses to the self-expression of the Church's faith, not as intending to report on actual events" (Wright, 2019, p. 92). A strong emphasis on the traditional use of the gospels for worship and private devotion has seemed to see them as not interested in Ranke's understanding of history as "of how it really was". This sceptical attitude has been greatly reinforced by how the gospels have played a prominent part in conversion to Christianity. Their proselytizing function has served to presume emotional bias in their writing without any concern for truth. This, of course, overlooks the fact that normally what promotes such bias is precisely concern for what is believed to be true.

See the next Chapter for further discussion of this powerful assumption in connection with the second historical principle, that of accepting the uniqueness of past events and the need to guard against the intrusion of hindsight.

(vi) Agenda-controlled

It is often assumed that if a person has a strong motive for writing that therefore what is written shows bias. Yet without motivation, is anything ever written? Also why, if there is enthusiasm for a cause, do we have to assume illegitimate prejudice on the part of the writer? Possible damaging bias does need to be guarded against, but to assume that people are always biased unacceptably betrays lack of trust in them as people. Moreover, to have strong opinions does not mean that they are not rationally based. Strongly held convictions involving passion may be the appropriate rational response to a particular circumstance.

A convincing example is given by Blomberg: "Some people, usually for anti-semitic purposes, deny or downplay the horrors of the Holocaust. But it has been the Jewish scholars who've created museums, written books, preserved artifacts, and documented eye witness testimony concerning the Holocaust. They have a very ideological purpose – namely, to ensure that such an atrocity never occurs again – but they have also been the most faithful and objective in their reporting of historical truth" (In Strobel, 2016, p. 33).

C.E. Hill discusses the opprobrium thrown at the second-century bishop Irenaeus of Lyons for the passionate language of his work *Against the Heresies*. He has been accused of banning diversity in a one-sided pro-Christianity crusade. The context of his writing, however, suggests a quite different view. He was writing a few years after the atrocities of 177 CE when Christians in Lyons and Vienne were accused of terrible crimes and brutally executed as a form of public entertainment. "The blistering accusations for which they died came from the Gospel of Judas which falsely accused them of Thyestian feasts – which refers to Greek mythology in which Thyestes ate his sons' flesh – and Oedipodean intercourse which refers to incest" (2010, p. 54).

Hill makes the ironic point that modern anti-establishment protests in favour of tolerance and diversity, and therefore of accepting the Gospel of Judas, really are being the opposite themselves of tolerant. "Whatever else might be said about the people behind this book, they can hardly be held up as models of religious toleration and the acceptance of 'alternative lifestyles'" (2010, p. 54).

Strobel offers another such example of the unenlightened nature of the apocryphal gospels: "The Gospel of Thomas ends with a note saying: 'Let Mary go away from us, because women are not worthy of life'. Jesus is quoted as saying: 'Lo, I shall lead her in order to make her a male, so that she too may become a living spirit, resembling you males. For every woman who makes herself male will enter the kingdom of heaven'" (Strobel, 2016, p. 72). Is this in support of transgender rights?

(vii) Conspiracy theory

What has been said about the agenda-controlled assumption is close to the presumption that those in authoritative positions will automatically seek to conserve their power: they will elbow out any rivals, placing suspicion rather than trust in the driving seat. Hill has done detailed research into what is described as the Great Gospel Conspiracy. According to this theory there were a great many gospels in the first centuries following Jesus, but the Church chose those that promoted its own causes, arrogantly throwing out competitors. Excitement following the discovery in 2006 of the Gospel of Judas received huge media attention. It seemed to support those academics who believed in "a hypnotic conspiracy featuring nefarious forces that 'hacked down' a forest of suppressed Gospels in favour of a politically-motivated canon of four" (2010, p. 245).

Hill's careful sifting of the evidence has shown up quite how unhistorical are the arguments for this theory. It seems that neither individuals nor councils created the canon; instead, they came to recognise and acknowledge the self-authenticating quality of these writings, which imposed themselves as canonical upon the church. Hill comments: "They almost seem to have chosen themselves through some sort of 'natural selection'" (2010 p. 229).

We live in an age when conspiracy theories are rife regarding, for example, the source of the Covid-19 pandemic. Any presumed conspiracy should emerge, however, from study of the evidence, not from a pre-acknowledged hostility to the institution, country or people seeking to protect their power.

This presumption applied to gospel research is dependent also on the hindsight with which scholars have tended to approach the gospels. They know what happened later instead of taking the evidence applicable at the time. See the next chapter for further discussion of this.

(viii) Orality

The disdain with which we, in our highly literate culture, may view the oral handing down of tradition needs to be challenged. To imagine that something remembered and told to others is simply invented is not justified. Williams notes: "The period of approx. the first 2 centuries is commonly known within Judaism as the *tannaitic* period, named after the *tannaim,* plural of tanna, meaning one who memorised and taught the tradition of the oral law. Rabbinic confidence in memorisation was so high that some rabbis even banned the writing of oral traditions" (2018, p. 99). Rabbis became famous for memorising the whole Torah, even as today many Muslims can repeat the whole of the Quran from memory.

Contemporary research into how tradition is handed down in oral communities indicates, as James Dunn in *The Oral Gospel Tradition* (2013) shows, that it is like and unlike at the same time. The point of the telling is to reinforce the tradition, but the way in which it is put across must vary according to the particular situation in which a person is speaking and others are listening. In this way the tradition remains fresh and active. The point of telling a story is to preserve the tradition. To treat what is remembered orally as free creation is wide of the mark.

Richard Bauckham has made an impressive case for considering that behind the writing of the gospels lies eyewitness testimony. He considers: "the implications of putting eyewitnesses back into the picture, not merely as the original sources of the gospel traditions, but as people who remained accessible sources and authoritative guarantors of their own testimony through the period between Jesus and the writing of the Gospels" (2006, p. 241).

Initially there undoubtedly would be many eyewitnesses regarding much that was claimed that Jesus said and did. In time, however, their number would dwindle for reasons of age and geography. Teaching about Jesus spread rapidly throughout Palestine and the Mediterranean world. Some eyewitnesses are likely to have travelled, but they would travel to different places. Therefore, I think that whilst Bauckham is correct in acknowledging the importance of eyewitness relevance regarding the truth of what was said about Jesus, we should not put unjustified reliance on it.

This is where Dunn's work on the overall reliability of oral evidence is so important. Dunn notes that Bauckham is basically correct in assuming the presence of eyewitnesses within the early church. Obvious examples he notes are Bartimeaus, Simon of Cyrene and the women at Jesus' tomb. We need to recognise, however, that: "the first disciples could not provide an authoritative check on the use made of the Jesus tradition in more than a few churches....Within 25 or 30 years little churches (house churches, apartment congregations, tenement groups) had spread widely throughout the north-eastern quadrant of the Mediterranean." Dunn maintains that, nevertheless, with or without explicit eyewitness support, "the tradition that has come down to us ... was assumed to retain the character and substance and variability of the tradition as first articulated by the earliest disciples" (2013, pp. 224f). Both Dunn and Bauckham acknowledge a clear example of where eyewitness testimony is not present, namely when Matthew changes the name of the tax-collector Levi to Matthew, as mentioned above.

To regard oral tradition with initial scepticism is not rationally justified. A major reason for such scepticism will be discussed in the next chapter. This chapter has shown indeed that, from a rational point of view, the seven other sources of suspicion against the gospels do not stand up either. Scepticism needs evidence; it cannot and should not be assumed.

Chapter 6

The Uniqueness of Historical Events:
2nd Historical Principle

This chapter will look at a second basic principle for historical research which has important implications for how research into Jesus has been conducted. Here I want to explore the importance for the historian that what happened in the past is always unique. I shall not devote a whole chapter to arguing for it because, once stated, it appeals to straightforward common sense. An anachronism, once seen as such, is obviously historically unjustified.

The Uniqueness of historical events

The basic unit to be explored in history is human behaviour. This can never be set out in inflexible and therefore absolutely certain principles. Rather it is the case that people behave in uniquely different ways. The distinguished historian and philosopher Isaiah Berlin gives a particular example. If someone reported that at the Battle of Austerlitz Napoleon wore an old-style three-cornered hat instead of the usual two-cornered hat, this could not be dismissed by saying this was unusual so it is unlikely to have happened. The whole point is that *because* it was unusual it was remarked upon and found its way into the record of the battle.

As Berlin expressed it in a rather difficult but nevertheless crucially important passage for understanding the nature of history: "If a historian were to attempt to cast doubt on – or explain away – some piece of individual observation of a type not otherwise suspect, say, that Napoleon had been seen in a three-cornered hat at a given moment during the battle of Austerlitz; and if the historian did so solely because he put his faith, for whatever reason, in a theory or law according to which French generals or heads of state never wore three-cornered hats during battles, his method, one can safely assert, would not meet with universal or immediate recognition from his profession. Any procedure designed to discredit the testimony of normally reliable witnesses or documents as, let us say, lies or forgeries, or as being defective at the very point at which the report about Napoleon's hat occurred, would be liable to be regarded as itself suspect, as an attempt to alter the facts to fit a theory" (in Hardy, 1997, under the heading 'The Concept of Scientific History', p. 27).

In this respect History is very different from Science, as discussed in Chapter 3. History is literally unrepeatable; what happened in the past cannot be broken up into analysable units and subjected to objective tests. Science looks for general laws, that is, for what is universal and happens all the time. History, on the other hand, has to try to discover what happened only once. The uniqueness of historical events must therefore never be forgotten. Napoleon's hat would never have been mentioned unless on a particular occasion he did something different from usual. So, to argue that generally something else would have been the case is strictly beside the point.

Chapter 8 will discuss an example of how this principle has been forgotten regarding a long passage argued by Ehrman as discounting the truth of what the gospels say about the resurrection of Jesus.

Berlin hints at why remembering the uniqueness of events is an important principle for interpretation. It is a standing temptation for historians to try to make their accounts fit their own agendas instead of the other way round: the result of dispassionate study should enable one's previous understanding to be modified in the light of research, not the other way round. Normally one can see the lack of this principle at work in what an opponent comes up with. A strongly partisan Republican view of the English Civil

War would be quick to see a non-historical reading of, say, the execution of Charles I by a royalist who had failed to be careful to show evidence for the interpretation given.

The danger of the intrusion of hindsight

An especial danger lies in using hindsight to interpret the past. Thomas Paine's remarks referred to in Chapter 1 about Jesus never writing a book is a hugely obvious example of failing to understand the historical context. He was simply seeing the past in terms of modern assumptions and realities: an illegitimate use of hindsight. The presumption of the inadequacy of oral evidence, discussed in the last chapter, is another more sophisticated example of hindsight playing its tricks.

In particular, the historian needs to exercise great caution not to allow the actions and roles of countries, institutions, groups and individuals to be viewed in the light of later developments. Just because a country became an aggressor in a war does not mean that its whole history should be tarred with the same brush. Instead, the historian's proper role is to seek to uncover the precise causes of the later behaviour, so that the earlier history of that country can be allowed to stand in its own right.

A reputation arising out of later circumstances should not be allowed to distort investigation into what happened earlier. Many people, for example, experience difficulty in listening to and appreciating the music of Wagner because they see it through the lens of its popularity with Hitler. It is necessary for people to lay aside this later history of its role in promoting the Third Reich, and see the cluster of ideas at work on Wagner during his lifetime: the need for Germany to find its own identity after the Napoleonic takeover, the possibilities of the whole Romantic movement in the arts, Wagner's achievement in brilliant orchestral writing, the emotional power of using the human voice as in opera etc., etc.

Inappropriate use of hindsight occurs when an earlier

period is presumed to be like a later period and found wanting if it is not. It is particularly easy for current concerns which arouse strong emotions to find people to blame in the past. As already mentioned in Chapter 3, the virtue signalling of today is committing a cardinal historical sin in judging people who lived in a very different climate of opinion according to present-day perceptions. Current concerns to blacken the reputation of Clive Rhodes of Oriel College, Oxford, or David Hume of Edinburgh University, demanding the removal of statues to them and other reminders of their name, betray a serious lack of historical understanding. Such people must be seen in context, according to the mindset of the times in which they lived. It is especially important to remember that they did not know what we now know: what stemmed from their actions. They were necessarily as ignorant of the actual consequences of their decisions as we are today of what we do or fail to do. Equally they were limited by a huge number of constraints, as we are today. If this is not understood and the warnings from past behaviour heeded, repetition in the future is more than likely. Ignorance is not a solution.

The impact of ignoring this historical principle in research into the gospels

(i) Hindsight inappropriately used

Hindsight constitutes an especial danger for those seeking to understand the first-century Palestinian conditions in which Jesus lived. The temptation is to use knowledge of what materialized later as a key to understanding what was earlier. But this presumes a close and justified causality for which clear evidence should be given, not assumed. In general, scholars seem to have been so enamoured of the Jesus fashioned by Christian belief of later centuries that concern for the original Jesus has tended to become obscure. They know what happened later instead of taking the evidence applicable at the time when Jesus was alive. After all, the Church did not exist in Jesus' time. Jesus has to be understood first without reference to the Church.

A cardinal example of this tendency of hindsight being inappropriately used is exposed by C.E. Hill in the Great Gospel Conspiracy discussed in the last chapter. This theory started with anger and irritation at what the Church in later centuries was regarded as becoming, namely an oppressive authority structure. These characteristics which were found reprehensible in a later period were then read back into the early period of formation.

Of course, the historian must use insights from her/his own time; we cannot undo knowledge of more recent developments, and in the interpretative task of historians, such knowledge can and must be used. But with a caution namely, that of being aware that evidence from a later period does not necessarily apply to an earlier period. Causality cannot be presumed.

The gospel-authors' presumed non-historical approach

Another very widespread example of challengeable use of hindsight relates to the suspicion that in no sense can the gospels be referred to as biography. Much has been made of the gospels not being properly presented as a modern biography would be, acknowledging sources adequately and with a clear chronology. They do not come up to standards of academic excellence promoted in later times. The Form Critical approach tended to refer to the gospels as a string of pearls giving the impression that they are merely separate anecdotes.

From this presumed defect of the gospels, a further deduction has been drawn, namely, that the Evangelists had no interest in writing history. The word gospel refers to "good news", not to any attempted truthful account of the life of Jesus. Viewing Jesus from the perspective afforded by hindsight has therefore had a lot to do with why much modern scholarship has viewed the gospels as primarily community documents. A strong emphasis on the traditional use of the gospels for worship and private devotion has seemed to indicate little interest in what Ranke called "how it really was".

Bultmann's understanding of the gospels as "primarily witnesses to self-expression of the church's faith", already quoted, was an important herald of this approach. It has been widely adopted by both religious and non-religious scholars. As one example out of so many that could be quoted, Dennis Nineham's commentary on *The Gospel of St Mark* (1963) is heavily dependent on this approach. He notes: "The older view that the Gospels were attempted biographies of Jesus, as adequate as the education of the Evangelists and the circumstances of the time would allow, has given place to the recognition that each of them was produced to meet some specific and practical needs in the church of its origin, and that it is those needs which have very largely controlled each Evangelist's choice, arrangement and presentation of material and distribution of emphasis" (p. 29). He can therefore sound a very sceptical note concerning the historicity of any gospel passages. See also the quotation given in Chapter 4 from the present-day theologian Eric Eve which is in line with this approach.

Such a view emerged from perceiving the role of the gospels in the church in later periods as concerned with worship, devotion, building up the community and proselytising. Continuity with how the Church developed over centuries became the leading guideline. Instead of trying to see Jesus in his historical context which was decidedly pre-Church, pre-worship of him, pre-proselytising, pre-building up a community, characteristics of a later period were placed onto the earlier period. The fact that the gospels have played a prominent part in conversion to Christianity does not deny their truth. That they were made-up propaganda requires proof; without evidence offered it is simply sceptical bias at work.

Distrust of oral transmission

This is another factor at work, for which hindsight is in part responsible. James Dunn in *The Oral Gospel Tradition* (2013) has shown how the hold of our literate society has made it difficult really to get on the wavelength of a pre-literate society. It tends to be assumed that its concern for truth was nebulous because not so sophisticated in the methods at its disposal as that of a literate society. This impacted powerfully on the approach to resolve the Synoptic Problem which was seen as dependent upon finding the original written version of a saying or event. This was deemed to provide the essential clue to understanding who Jesus was in his own time.

Even when the necessity for and importance of oral tradition was acknowledged by scholars, the assumption of the superiority of written sources over oral still was in evidence. Oral transmission tended to be treated *as though* it was written, assuming that there was one original from which later variants deviated.

This was the cardinal defect of the Form Critical approach discussed in Chapter 2. This sought to remove the layers of later orality to reach the original. This is a respected aim when dealing with written material, but it gives a false impression as to how knowledge is passed on orally. For it assumes that there is just one original form when in fact there probably were many forms right from the beginning. To assume that Jesus only said something once is highly improbable. Each time, different people would remember what he said differently, so that there never was an original which can be neatly recovered by the historian. Realisation of this eventually challenged reliance on the Form Critical approach.

Scholars would not today dream of making such a mistake of ignoring oral transmission, yet confidence in what is written down rather than what is transmitted orally is still with us. It is often assumed orally transmitted material is highly likely to be changed, whilst the written word remains constant. The written word has a definiteness about it which oral transmission lacks. What is said verbally cannot be monitored and challenged in the same rigorous way as what is written down.

Distrust of oral transmission is, however, not justified. In fact, the level of concern for truth in oral-dominated societies can be very impressive as discussed in the last chapter. Moreover, it is noteworthy that 80–90 % of Jesus' words recorded in the gospels are in poetic form, using such memory aids as metre, balanced lines, parallelism, etc. This shows that Jesus was clearly aware of the importance of memory. People did not automatically write down notes in those days and then regard them with something akin to a binding authority, as we tend to do today in our exceedingly literate age.

It is a mark of inadmissible hindsight at work. Without giving initial benefit of doubt to what is remembered as well as to what is written, no knowledge of any kind becomes possible. To assume inaccuracies requires reasons in support.

(ii) Search for reliable criteria with its implied analogy with science for testing validity of a text

In the wake of the gospels failing to satisfy critics regarding the eight problems perceived in Chapter 5, many scholars have presumed that everything the gospels say must be subject to a series of tests before it can be accepted as likely to be true. Such methodological criteria appear to offer an opportunity for definite, quasi-scientific reasoning in facing the question of whether anything in the gospels is reliable. The seemingly cut-and-dried nature of these tools gives an impression of objective enquiry.

The Criteria for Authenticity

A large number of such criteria have been put forward. See e.g., Stanley. E. Porter, *The Criteria for Authenticity in Historical-Jesus Research: Previous Discussion & New Proposals* (2000). Debate about criteria for authenticity spans the quests. Porter's book makes a thorough study of them and suggests three further criteria.

Some of the criteria put forward are of a general kind without applying which no history could be pursued. Thus, that of Coherence/Consistency seeks to ensure that a saying or event fits in with other sayings and deeds already established as authentic. Another criterion concerns Historical Plausibility. This is a wide-ranging appeal to what makes sense which is involved in all historical interpretation.

A further criterion which is obviously helpful is that of Palestinian Environment relating to appropriate context. Accuracy of detail does show that a purported saying or event comes from the right period and location. Serious mistakes, such as using names associated with a different place and time from when the incident is purported to have taken place, does indeed promote well-founded doubt. This is the case regarding the pseudo-gospels such as the Gospel of Judas (see Hill, 2010, pp. 53–5).

Concerning the other criteria, it may in general be said that they can be helpful if considered in a positive sense, but exceedingly unhelpful if used in a negative sense. This is well illustrated by that of Multiple Attestation. If there is more than one reference to a saying or event, this can indeed provide extra certainty concerning the truth of what happened; if a saying or event occurs in many different places, it can give even greater confidence concerning its veracity. Applied negatively, however, such that the text is viewed with caution or disbelief *unless* there is multiple attestation, this criterion is clearly false. It would discredit most of history.

Here is an example of how the negative application of this

criterion fails. Ehrman states: "If a story – a saying, a deed of Jesus – is found in only one source, it cannot be corroborated independently, and so it is less likely to be authentic"(2014, p. 96). This is assuming the correctness of a sceptical stance. Moreover, it is simply unjustified. Just because a piece of information appears on its own does not mean it is necessarily false. As Boyd notes: "Most of ancient history is based on single sources" (in Strobel, 2016, p. 127).

Furthermore, multiple attestation provides no guarantee of truth in any case. It can be attributed to collusion, or to one person copying from another. Such practices do not argue for authenticity but possibly for its opposite. Mistakes and misunderstandings can be passed on via copying and constant repetition. It is to be noted that in academic circles this presents a real danger unintentionally encouraged indeed by the peer-review system operating in academic journals. This procedure is intended as a means of maintaining high standards. It can, however, easily promote conformity with what is currently fashionable when would-be contributors do not wish to risk not being published because they are thinking outside the box. It is remarkably difficult to find in some journals any comment challenging major assumptions normally voiced in that journal.

A major criterion has been that of dissimilarity either with what was typical of the Jewish culture and times in which Jesus lived or with the early Church. Perrin describes the criterion of dissimilarity thus: "The earliest form of a saying we can reach may be regarded as authentic if it can be shown to be dissimilar to characteristic emphases both of ancient Judaism and of the early Church."

This can easily imply that if it is similar, it is not to be trusted. It is important to note that scholars do not usually say that a saying or event could be false unless it meets this criterion. Phrasing it as Perrin does, however, tends to favour doubt unless it does fit this criterion. It is an assumption that can creep in uninvited when the door is opened.

Applied to the Jewishness of Jesus, this criterion turns Jesus into a cardboard figure instead of a person actually living in first-century Palestine. As a Jew, he was bound to reveal his Jewishness in so many ways. Similarly, regarding dissimilarity with later Christian development, the early Church grew out of respect and worship of Jesus, so to presume that there was no link between what Jesus taught and did with what the first Christians believed is impossible to defend. Dunn summarises: "It is inevitable that since the criterion of dissimilarity is the primary sieve, the use of these criteria will present us with a Jesus who is dissimilar to and distinct from the Jesus of the earliest Christians ... this must be a wrong-headed approach." Today few scholars would defend either way of understanding the criterion of dissimilarity; the impact over decades, however, of trying to use these criteria has been exceedingly damaging.

A variant criterion is that of embarrassment. The authenticity of such events as Jesus' confessions of ignorance as to the future, his despairing cry on the cross, the disciples' flight after Jesus' arrest, Peter's denial and so forth can therefore be acknowledged as high. No one who acknowledged the crucial role of Peter in the formation of the Christian Church would have been likely to make up Jesus' strong rebuke to Peter: "Get thee behind me, Satan." Yet to argue that unless a saying or event would cause embarrassment to the Church it is likely to be doubtful, would appear to be odd. This is another example of how a criterion understood in a positive sense may be valid, but negatively may not make sense.

These criteria of dissimilarity have been responsible for many blind alleys in research. As Dunn states, this has provided one of the most important methodological principles underlying the quest for the historical Jesus for nearly 50 years. A particular example occurs in the way in which Christian prophecy, a feature of early Christian communities, was seen by some scholars as a substitute for genuine sayings of Jesus which appear in the gospels. Kasemann, the founder of the Second Quest, stated that: "[C]ountless 'I' sayings of the Christ who revealed himself through the mouth of prophets gained entry into the Synoptic tradition as sayings of Jesus"(quoted by Dunn, 2013, p. 14). Kasemann considered, for example, that Mark 8:38 reflects 1 Cor 3:17 and Gal 1:9.

Dunn deals with this suspected phenomenon extensively (see 2013, pp. 15ff). He acknowledges both that Christian prophecy did occur in the early Church, and that a passage like Matthew 18:20: "Where two or three are gathered together in my name, there am I in the midst of them," reflects a post-Easter situation: one in which an ecstatic Christian prophet could have spoken. This does not, however, warrant the wholesale assumption that presumed sayings of Jesus in the gospels actually go back to early Christian prophets.

Dunn, in fact, offers historical evidence that the prophetic sayings of Christian prophecy were subjected to considerable critique and not taken as automatically valid even at the time of their utterance. The early Christians, like students of the Jewish prophetic tradition before them, knew plenty about false prophecy and they guarded against it (see, especially, Dunn, 2013, pp. 18–40). The likelihood therefore of their finding a place in the gospels is not based on historical facts but on conjecture.

In conclusion, we can agree with sceptical scholars such as Lataster who consider that many of the Criteria of authenticity are "contradictory, redundant and speculative. With regard to their application by Biblical historians, use of the Criteria can often be inconsistent and inadequate" (2015, p. 66). He quotes Porter's comment: "Each of them seems subject to valid criticism" (2015, p. 68f). These criteria are only rationally valid if stated in a positive form.

In themselves they are questionable as criteria for answering doubt. So, even before attempting to apply these criteria to the gospels, they are found wanting. This means that any case based on them for scepticism towards the gospel fails rationally before it has started. The findings of the Jesus Seminar (see above in Chapters 2 and 4) based very much on such criteria, fail to take the principle of accepting the uniqueness of historical sayings and events seriously.

I now move on to a third required historical principle.

Chapter 7

Explanation of Major Facts: 3rd Historical Principle

It is easy to become so preoccupied with pursuing detailed clues that the purpose of the investigation as a whole can get lost. Searching for the most comprehensive explanation of the major facts behind an enquiry is crucial; the overall interpretation matters. The point of doing History is not to end up with a series of unconnected presumed facts.

Facts and interpretation

As Hunt argues: "Historical truth is two-tiered: facts are at issue in the first tier, interpretations in the second. Although it is possible to separate them for purposes of discussion, in the actual practice of history they turn out to be interlocking. A fact is inert until it is incorporated into an interpretation that gives it significance, and the power of an interpretation depends on its ability to make sense of the facts" (2018, p. 30).

Seeking to discover what the facts are at a microscopic level in the manner of a detective is necessary. To take the example of Obama's birth certificate again (see Chapter 4), the historian is justified in presuming that Obama was born on August 4, 1961, in Honolulu, Hawaii. Hunt points out that it is possible to imagine "that it was forged on an old typewriter using a blank old form or just produced with some kind of digital technique, but no evidence has been found to support any such conclusion". The facticity of such an explanation is therefore highly questionable; the date and place of Obama's birth remains a fact (2018, p. 32). Yet by itself, why does this matter? It became a political issue in light of its challenge by Donald Trump. It was part of a major reason why Obama was elected President of the US. It coloured his understanding of life and therefore his policies.

It is crucial not to lose sight of the fundamental reason for the enquiry as a whole. Work on details needs to help towards an explanation which satisfies all that we do know and also what we are enquiring further about. As Hunt points out, there are "core standards that are widely accepted among historians: the truthfulness of any interpretation depends on its coherence and its ability to offer an explanation for the important facts" (2018, p. 41).

She gives an example from her own experience of what such concern for the important facts involves. She cites her enquiry concerning whether Napoleon had a paternalistic attitude towards women. "To be as complete an explanation as possible, my emphasis must make sense of as many applicable facts as possible" (2018, p. 41). She notes that she does not need to expound on Napoleon's military strategies but she should take account of, for example, his laws. Discovering that these included forbidding a wife, without her husband's consent, to acquire property, contract debt, work, or make a will is very strong relevant evidence.

Searching for the most comprehensive explanation of major facts behind an enquiry

Five particular points should be borne in mind:

(i) Distinguishing between historical evidence and conjecture

The use of conjecture is unavoidable in working towards finding a true assessment of anything in history. However, it is especially important to be aware of where conjecture is properly suggested by the evidence and where it may have floated free of the evidence, or be operating in the absence of any evidence.

For this is the point at which prior opinion and commitment can most easily unjustifiably influence our assessment of the historical question of what actually happened.

Conjecture is closely associated with what people want to believe was true to support their current world view. It is easy for overall interpretation to be shackled to non-historical considerations as in the above objection to Obama's birth certificate. In this case conjecture had no evidence at all supporting it. To let ideology of any kind determine historical interpretation will not do. The results do not deserve to be considered history in any way.

Failure to distinguish between evidence-based interpretation and mere conjecture is especially serious in that, just because something *could* have happened, that is, that one can imagine it happening, does not mean that it *did* happen. This third historical principle therefore brings in especially the question of subjectivity and potential bias. Strong emotional commitment to a particular world view or to the importance of a particular insight can easily lead to a single-issue syndrome whereby one particular concern so dominates the scene that other equally relevant aspects are ignored. The choice for the single issue can be very subjective indeed. It can, for example, denigrate the phenomenon of the popular appeal of Captain Sir Tom Moore, who so captured the imagination of people with his creative approach during the coronavirus pandemic, as no more than an outbreak of white British supremacy. All the many reasons why such diverse people, globally as well as in Britain, found him an inspiration can be simply ignored.

(ii) Distinguishing between helpful and unhelpful bias

The word bias is interesting. It is often used in a negative sense. To accuse a historian of bias tends to imply criticism of what that person thinks. Yet it is also what none of us can avoid because it relates to our personal perspective on life. Hunt makes the important point:

"Since historians always write from points of view that are shaped by their personal histories and social contexts, their accounts cannot claim to be entirely objective. When I write on Napoleon, for example, I do so from the perspective of a white, middle-class, woman scholar trained in the US of the 1960s.... I am more likely than some to emphasise his efforts to thwart democratic impulses and ensure the subordination of women and children to husbands and fathers. But this positioning does not mean that my account is false, unless I go so far as to argue that these issues are the only ones that matter in considering Napoleon's record. The truest history is often written by people with deep commitments on one side or another of an issue." She quite rightly adds "Blandness is not the same thing as truth" (Hunt, 2018, p. 39f).

We need to remember therefore that those who criticise the views of others do so out of their own experience and understanding. To accuse an opponent of being biased is to use a boomerang which can as easily knock out one's own position.

The unavoidability of subjectivity does not mean that there are no safeguards against falsity. Historians need to be strictly as impartial as they can be, putting the search for truth above their own private and personal interests. Basil Mitchell describes what is needed: "It requires one to be scrupulous in assembling the evidence, honest in recognising arguments against one's position, fair in assessing the force of these arguments, sympathetic in representing the position of those with whom one disagrees. Academics all too often fail to satisfy these requirements, but failure nevertheless it is, and the requirements are absolute" (1994, p. 23f).

Mitchell is quite rightly very definite about this. Academics have a huge responsibility for promoting genuine dialogue. The failure of universities to challenge the woke culture is a very clear case in point. To give way to activists wishing to close down free speech to those with whom they disagree is an extraordinarily serious matter. This is not because freedom of speech should be preserved at all costs; there are many reasons why the West should not have over stressed this value. Speech can be not only hurtful to people in the sense of giving offence, but it can promote dangerous action. Freedom of speech is a relative, not an absolute, value. Its safe practice depends on many other values being in place, such as concern for justice and compassion.

Preventing those with whom we may disagree from having a voice is crucially anti-democratic. Discussion and debate are one of the major ways of seeking to reach truth. It is through the expression of points for and against a particular view or action that sound understanding of an issue is likely to emerge.

Traditionally universities have been the home of fearless debate going back, for example, right to the time of Abaelard in the twelfth century whose rigorous questioning opened up whole areas of new thinking. Therefore, for universities to close down the opportunity for debate represents a gross denial of one of their main purposes for existence. If universities stop being concerned about reaching knowledge and truth, what help are they to society as a whole?

I have developed this point at some length because in an era when many assume we live "post-truth", universities should be leading the way towards a more enlightened position. The woke culture can be seen as irrational on so many grounds that for universities not to be exposing this is a betrayal of what they stand for. To give way to a counter-culture of policing of speech is the exact opposite of what they should be doing. False notions can only be successfully challenged by reasoning if they are expressed. To refuse this is to drive false opinions further away than ever from rational discourse. This is especially relevant regarding research on the historical Jesus where preconceptions can so easily take over. Contrary views need to be expressed in order to be challenged.

The scholar needs to care about enquiry passionately and yet guard against the impact of unhelpful emotional reaction. It is especially important to be fair-minded to those who oppose one's views, so that such people and their views are not vilified but treated with respect and listened to properly. In this way a subjectivity which is compassionate towards others and concerned for trying to develop a common mind in interpretation is an aid not a hindrance.

(iii) Appeal to facts?

The accusation of bias cannot be avoided by pointing to facts, because these facts only land us in further trouble. For what do we call facts? How are they arrived at? Is not subjectivity involved in discovering them, formulating them, selecting them, arranging them, and in the conclusions drawn from them? Facts are very far from being straightforward. They can be false – just what someone chooses to proclaim as fact. A clear example is the confidence expressed concerning Anthropogenic Global Warming (AGW) that the "science is settled" when the scientific evidence for it is still contested by many scientists (see, e.g., Christopher Booker, *The Real Global Warming*, 2009).

Whatever views we may hold regarding the need to reduce carbon emissions with the implied vast changes to the economy that entails, scientists are not in fact agreed on the evidence put forward that such action is needed "to save the planet". The AGW movement is increasingly being seen as a political, and indeed almost a quasi-religious, movement in which its advocates appear in the role of saviours. How far the computer-dependent evidence put forward by bodies such as the IPCC in favour of this deserves to be treated with as much respect as the "hard evidence" which scientists have traditionally employed is an unresolved issue.

Any who question the current consensus have been, for a long time, described as *deniers* with its overtones of illicit Holocaust deniers; this suggests that emotion has been leading the way. Science proceeds normally in calm collaborative search for the evidence and its correct interpretation. It welcomes, rather than denigrating, scientists who put forward a contrary view. Einstein specifically invited criticism of his relativity theory. Presumed agreement on AGW occurred within a decade, and moreover one in which a new Ice Age had first been predicted. It is so easy for reasons for action to be presumed valid instead of being debated as accurately as possible.

Facts can also be used to disguise or keep out of consideration other facts, whether deliberately or not. For what is drawn attention to inevitably puts what is not drawn attention to into the background, maybe never to emerge. Discussing what can contribute to mental health, for example, can easily so revolve around purely humanly conceived remedies that any mention of the possibly positive impact of religious faith is left out. If the reason for this is argued along the lines of "we cannot presume that anyone has religious faith, whilst everyone is human, so by leaving religion out we are being truly inclusive," that may be so. It does not, however, alter the fact, and fact it is, that by never mentioning religion it is being hidden and becomes unavailable for consideration. The long-term effects of non-discussion of issues are serious.

Reform of education is seriously hampered, for example, if the importance of the arts is ignored. For these offer a most important way forward in connecting thinking with emotion, with the heart, that is, bringing together what educationalists refer to as the cognitive and the affective domains. An educated person should be someone able to be creative and not just operating like a computer or a robot with information fed into it. Treating the arts as Cinderella subjects on the curriculum by comparison with the STEM subjects limits education all round. Lack of exposure to the visual, dramatic and musical propensities which so powerfully delineate different cultures and civilisations prevents children and students from the opportunity of getting on their wavelength. No one can think about or develop an interest in what they have never heard. The same point applies very much to the importance of Religious Education in schools; as a Cinderella subject on the curriculum, religion cannot be taken seriously.

(iv) Perceiving coherence

Hunt sees this as a major feature of genuine historical understanding. Coherence is concerned with whether the pieces of the jigsaw puzzle which have survived fit together or appear to be at variance.

"A coherent account is logical; it cites evidence that is germane and does not draw irrational conclusions from that evidence. If I want to argue that Napoleon considered a paternalistic relationship to women and children essential to his brand of authoritarian regime, I will look for evidence in his laws, writings, and even his personal life, but I cannot maintain that the fact that he loved his wife shows he was paternalistic. Such a conclusion does not follow logically[....][H]e could have loved his wife and favoured any number of different regimes" (2018, p. 41).

To evaluate the correctness of Alfred the Great's reputation for learning, the truth or otherwise of the burning the cakes anecdote is not needed, nor details of his campaign against the Vikings and crucial victory at the battle of Edington, and so forth. What is relevant is his establishment of a court school to educate his own children, the sons of his nobles, and intellectually promising boys of lesser birth; an attempt to require literacy in those who held offices of authority, and his translations of works from Latin to English. Other considerations could also be relevant and dent his reputation if, for example, he portrayed the low level of learning which he inherited as far worse than it was and whether he really was not personally responsible for the four translations with which he is credited.

If, however, the enquiry was to see whether he deserved his title of "the Great", in order to adjudicate his overall reputation, even the story of his burning the cakes would be relevant; were it to be a myth, it would still show the high regard in which his character was held. It is difficult to imagine such a story being invented about Napoleon, for example. A generalisation can become questionable if only one instance of its not being true is encountered; one example of wanton cruelty would put a question mark beside a person's reputation for gentleness and benevolence to all.

Drawing up a coherent picture is thus very much ongoing work. Honesty in facing up to as much of the evidence as possible, including especially what may not serve one's own preferred view, is essential. Being selective in what we choose to notice is an especial danger associated with the single issue syndrome in which a specific focus is dominant. Over-concern for, let us say, gender equality can lead to ignoring many other factors which are real events such as people having identified themselves throughout history as male or female according to the reproductive functions which each person happens to have. As to why, nevertheless, women have been in almost all civilisations not treated as equal with men depends on a host of other factors such as sheer physical strength, the practical convenience of allocation of tasks, inherited preferences, the impact of particular teachings and individuals, and so forth. Ruling out of consideration the impact of any of these factors will not lead to a coherent understanding of the issue of gender equality. Rather, enquiry is likely to end up one-sided and biased in a pejorative sense of that word. An all-round view is needed, with the courage to question any factors which appear to be at variance with other factors. Trial and error will probably be needed to complete the jigsaw satisfactorily and not cheating by deliberately losing pieces which do not fit in!

(v) Concern for completeness

We need to ask whether our interpretation of precise details is creating a vacant place still to be filled regarding the enquiry as a whole. This exposes a question: what does the denying of something leave in its place? It is a question which refers both to the comprehensiveness of an interpretation by its not leaving out what would be relevant, and also to the obvious failure of an interpretation if it fails to offer any adequate explanation at all to the questions promoting the investigation in the first place.

In education the null curriculum is an important concept, namely, that we influence pupils profoundly not only by what is taught explicitly but by what is omitted, by what is never mentioned or discussed. An example has just been discussed in which education is deficient if it hardly mentions or encourages the pursuit of arts subjects. As a principle in the study of history this refers to considering the consequences of omitting relevant material, as well as reflecting on what is left unexplained if such and such a reading of particular details is accepted as correct.

This exposes a question: what does the denying of something leave? If we can trust no source material then it means we have to admit to knowing nothing about whatever it concerns. Take, for example, Caesar's *Gallic Wars*. Some may say that he wrote this work to support his overall ambitions, so we have to treat his narrative with suspicion. Yet, if we are to doubt its historical reliability, we must have superior evidence to dethrone reliance on the text which Caesar wrote. Thus, when he writes "The Germans differ much from these (Gallic) usages, for they have neither druids to preside over sacred offices, nor do they pay great regard to sacrifices," on what basis can this assertion be challenged? (Book 6 Chapter 21 trans. W.A. McDevitta & W.S. John). If archaeological remains are uncovered showing clear signs that druids were operating in German areas prior to Caesar's invasion then, and only then, is it appropriate to question Caesar's truthfulness on this matter. The fact that many people, then as now, regard him as personally ambitious and capable of writing deliberate fraud or, at any rate, of grossly exaggerating how much he had achieved, cannot by itself invalidate what he wrote. The critic must supply evidence that the text is faulty. It is related to the basic principle that just because people *can* be dishonest it does not mean that they *are* on any precise occasion.

In this instance, that we can know nothing about the existence of the druids in Germanic lands except for what Caesar says, we may happily say "so be it"; it is not a matter of fundamental importance. Ignorance is not, however, an acceptable alternative to trying to search for truth on matters of great importance. Ignorance of the American Indians who already lived in the land conquered by Christopher Columbus has resulted in terrible wrong thinking and social injustice. We might almost argue that such ignorance is culpable for it helped to create a serious situation. Again, ignorance concerning the slave trade, and also of contemporary examples of gross lack of human rights to workers, is exceedingly grave. Who can say that such knowledge does not matter?

Claiming that we cannot know anything reliable about X in practice can open the door to legions of un-investigated fillers-in. People can just posit what they like. This is not just a light-hearted matter; it can have very grave consequences. Roger Boyes, in *The Times* October 10, '20 under the title "Neo-Nazis are still fired up by the myth of Hitler's great escape", sums up the dangerous effect of believing that Hitler did not die in his bunker at the end of WWII. He notes: "Historians do have to stand up and present solid evidence, be honest when history is incomplete and face down those who are trying to insert palpable nonsense into the public domain." He then refers to Richard Evans's new book *The Hitler Conspiracies* which shows how that can be done, informed by the work of a multi-disciplined team at Cambridge University. This is directly relevant to the search for the historicity of Jesus because, as will be discussed in the next chapter, non-explanation for the existence of Christianity can open the door to wild notions.

The search for historical truth is always ongoing

We can conclude this chapter therefore by noting with Hunt that "the benchmarks of true facts, coherence and completeness offer a surprisingly wide opening for historical expression" (2018, p. 50). Yet it must always be remembered that "Even when a historical interpretation is based upon true facts, is logically coherent and as complete as a scholar can make it, the truth of that interpretation remains provisional. New facts can be discovered and the benchmark for completeness shifts over time" (2018, p. 54). Our knowledge is always partial but is not just fiction.

Searching for the most comprehensive explanation of the major facts behind an enquiry involves holistic awareness. Ranke had a broad and inclusive approach to the question of knowledge. Thus, he wrote "Two qualities, I think, are required for the making of the true historian: first he must feel a participation and pleasure in the particular for itself.... Still, this does not suffice; the historian must keep his eye on the universal aspect of things" (in Stern, p. 59). Ranke is asking for the same qualities of balance with are needed so much of the time in life generally. In music, for example, the performer must give precise attention to the note being played at this moment. Yet if that is all that is attended to, there will be no music, only a succession of notes. For music requires the ongoing movement which makes sense of the individual notes. So, the musician has to acknowledge that both this note and what it is part of matter equally.

Iain McGilchrist has written a remarkably relevant book drawing on insights from neuroscience on the two hemispheres of the brain (*The Master and His Emissary: The Divided Brain and the Making of the Western World*, 2009). He notes that the left hemisphere (LH) and the right hemisphere (RH) work together, and are both needed for human functioning. They do so, however, in crucially different ways.

The left hemisphere is logical, articulate, critical, focussing on a part and concerned with detail; moreover, it looks for general laws and is naturally sympathetic to a scientific approach to knowledge. The right hemisphere is concerned with the whole not just parts. It is holistic, affirming, naturally artistic and accepting of uniqueness. Its use of language far exceeds just literalism. It is aware of paradox and of how difficult it is to reach consistency when the whole of experience is considered.

McGilchrist thinks the West needs "a complete change of heart and mind", because it has over-valued LH thinking and has neglected the RH. This is critical because whilst the RH can include the LH concerns within its overall approach, the LH cannot reciprocate. To pursue its function of preciseness it necessarily has to exclude, deliberately, what cannot be neatly measured. The relationship between the two hemispheres needs to be the reverse of what generally has happened in the West, and this relates to the title of McGilchrist's book. The LH, because of its focus on precision, makes a good servant but a bad master, for it is incapable of understanding the RH. The RH on the other hand can appreciate what the LH can offer and use it accordingly. The RH therefore should be the Master. The LH is the natural home of an either/or mentality, whilst the RH prefers both/and thinking. The LH is hard-edged and wants to control and manage, whilst the RH wants to collaborate and be generous minded. The LH is ideal for finding out about things;

the RH ideal for learning about persons.

If the search for details encourages left-hemisphere thinking, the search for overall explanation which places the details unearthed into a picture frame which gives them meaning requires above all right-hemisphere thinking. A narrow scientific exploration will not do. Interpretation demands that evidence is looked at in the round. If the holistic view is denied, the purpose of history making sense of the past into the present is lost. The next chapter will show how that applies very much to the search for the Jesus of history.

Chapter 8

The Problem of Non-Explanation

How far have the quests for the historical Jesus offered a historically convincing explanation for the overall purpose of the enquiry: to discover what can be reliably known about Jesus and the start of the movement which led to the existence of Christianity? The latter is a supremely well-attested fact, so failure to offer a plausible account of how it originated would be a grave indictment of the historical investigation.

John Dominic Crossan, perhaps the most influential member of the Jesus Seminar, notes the astonishing diversity of views on who the historical Jesus was. He commented in *The Historical Jesus* (1991): "But that stunning diversity is an academic embarrassment. It is impossible to avoid the suspicion that historical Jesus research is a very safe place to do theology and call it history, to do autobiography and call it biography." This is not a promising finding; it has the effect of burying all scholars under a blanket of illicit subjectivity.

Many contemporary views of Jesus do indeed reflect the values of the scholars expressing them. Thus, Dunn notes that the Neo-Liberal Jesus has returned. "It is a Jesus who could well be imagined in many a twentieth century faculty staff room or as an independent 'loose cannon' academic." He notes, for example, that Crossan ended up with "'a peasant Jewish cynic', calling for a radical egalitarianism and proclaiming 'the broker-less kingdom of God', and Marcus Borg with 'a teacher of culturally subversive wisdom'" (2003, p. 58ff).

Is there any way in which scholars can be brought together in agreement? All scholars may concur that the rise of Christianity was due to what happened after Jesus' death: his resurrection. It is hard to refute this because the evidence for it is so strong.

This does not help much, however, because the dependence of Christianity upon the resurrection of Jesus is interpreted in very different ways. Many scholars are sceptical of it as a historical event as discussed in Chapter 3. So, appeal to it by itself does not lead us forward. There is more to say, however, about alternative explanations of the resurrection. Reasoning still has a crucial role to play. Are all or any of the alternatives to seeing the resurrection as a historical happening actually valid?

Evidence for the non-historicity of the Resurrection of Jesus as an event

It is highly significant that, as discussed in Chapter 6, none of the theories accounting for the resurrection of Jesus as humanly fabricated can claim the universal assent of other sceptical scholars. Crucially, moreover, none have historical evidence supporting them. Instead, the sceptical case rests heavily on psychological explanations for the resurrection, on the notion that the early disciples had visions to hallucinatory experiences. Ludemann focusses on the leaders of the new movement, Peter and Paul, considering that they were both suffering trauma and therefore vulnerable to fantasy.

As leadership is hugely important in establishing new movements, it may be appropriate to consider Ludemann's case more fully. Once again, however, there is the difficulty of finding any historical evidence. For a detailed review of the evidence see William Lane Craig "Visions of Jesus: A Critical Assessment of Gerd Lüdemann's Hallucination Hypothesis" https://www.reasonablefaith.org. Is it nothing more than surmising that Peter's resurrection viewing was "all in his mind"? Was it perhaps a brilliant way of overcoming his mental distress at the way in which he had denied knowing Jesus before his crucifixion? Was he summoning up all he knew about body-and-soul relationship and concluding it does not matter that Jesus is dead – his spirit lives on?

Such psychological musings are not even psychologically persuasive if thought about. Here is a man of forceful character and courageous leadership qualities who had just witnessed the horrific death of his hero. He had, moreover, no means of knowing that Jesus' disciples might not also be pursued to the death; he had been so frightened before Jesus was finally convicted, indeed, that he denied even knowing his master three times. It is almost certain that psychologically such a man would not be capable at that time of any inner capacity for self-healing and for intellectual reflection on body-and-soul relationship. Would not a real event have been needed to transform such a man? This is precisely what the gospels claim happened. Gary Habermas, moreover, considers that Ludemann fails to diagnose correctly the true problem Peter faced. It was not so much that he had failed his Lord as that his Lord had failed him! He had been following a failed Messianic pretender (2005).

Ludemann applies his psychological approach to Paul also. Habermas, however, argues that the evidence suggests that Paul the Pharisee did not struggle with a guilt complex under the Jewish law. The Swedish theologian Krister Stendhal wrote: "Contrast Paul, a very happy and successful Jew, one who can ... say..., 'As to the righteousness under the law, (I was) blameless' (Philippians 3:6). That is what he says. He experiences no troubles, no problems, no qualms of conscience. He is a star pupil, the student to get the thousand dollar graduate scholarship in Gamaliel's Seminary...."(1963, pp. 199–215).

That some scholars have thought that Paul was guilt ridden is an indication also of their failing to acknowledge the second historical principle, that of the uniqueness of history. Stendhal pointed out that Western readers have the tendency to interpret Paul in light of Martin Luther's struggles with guilt and sin. The Reformation gave huge significance to the notion of justification by faith and the need to avoid the least dependence on human good works as a means to gaining salvation. The letters of Paul, and particularly that of Romans, were understood as supporting this view. Such exegesis illicitly views the past through the lens of hindsight. Larry Hurtado commented that Bultmann "approached the ancient Christian texts with a theological criterion, a particular formulation of justification by faith, which he used to judge whether the writings were valid or not"(in Longenecker et al., 2014). It is noteworthy that Schweitzer back in 1912 had made the same point in a very acerbic manner: "Reformation exegesis read its own ideas into Paul, in order to receive them back again clothed with Apostolic authority" (1912, p. 2). This relates clearly to an ideological position, and by itself does not constitute historical reasoning.

Failure of support from historical evidence is the kiss of death for sceptical theories explaining the resurrection of Jesus. For how rational is it that scholars who have insisted on the most rigorous application of criticism to the evidence actually put forward in the gospels should defend alternative explanations which are not historically evidenced? It is time to consider what can claim such evidence, namely, the evidence in the gospels.

Evidence for the resurrection of Jesus as a historical event

The gospels in fact give impressive evidence. It includes the empty tomb, the experience of the women visiting it, the viewings of Jesus by many people on different occasions, the teaching of the early church and the willingness of prime eyewitnesses to risk death rather than deny this. Back in 1846, Simon Greenleaf, a principal founder of the Harvard Law School who wrote *The Testimony of the Evangelists Examined by the Rules of Evidence Administered in Courts of Justice*, was quoted in Chapter 5 defending the integrity of the gospels. He summed up his argument thus:

"Let the witnesses be compared with themselves, with each other, and with the surrounding facts and circumstances; and let their testimony be sifted, as if it were given in a court of justice, on the side of the adverse party, the witnesses being subjected to a rigorous cross-examination. The result, it is confidently believed, will be an undoubting conviction of their integrity, ability and truth ... Either the men of Galilee were men of superlative wisdom, and extensive knowledge and experience, and of deeper skill in the arts of deception, than any and all others, before or after them, or they have truly stated the astonishing things which they saw and heard" (quoted in Strobel, Ibid. pp. 46 & 53).

Here he makes an important and largely neglected point. If the gospel evidence is discredited, the alternative is equally unbelievable. That from such humble and unexpected circumstances, a major movement would begin extending throughout the world for two millennia which still shows no signs of abating globally.

Many initially sceptical scholars have, after examining the evidence, become convinced of its truth: for example, another lawyer Frank Morison described in detail in *Who Moved the Stone?* what impressed him so much (1987). Similarly, the investigative journalist Strobel, already quoted, rigorously interviewed leading Christians and, as he said, "took a step of faith in the same direction the evidence was pointing" (2016, p. 278).

The problem is, however, that many scholars do not accept the strength of the case, as we have seen in previous chapters. Even a moderate scholar such as Géza Vermes, who is clearly driven by great empathy and respect for Jesus, cannot accept that the gospel evidence is trustworthy. The final sentence in his book *Jesus the Jew* speaks of the "mesmerizing presence of the teaching and example of the real Jesus" (p. 444), yet he is resolute in denial of the resurrection of Jesus (See, e.g., pp. 398–404; 433–441).

Appeal to the gospel evidence appears, for the sceptical scholar, to be caught in a circularity of mistaken memory, perhaps deliberate deception and/or mythological embellishment. So, according to these scholars, the resurrection of Jesus did not happen. They do not deny that the resurrection of Jesus must feature in any explanation for the rise of Christianity. They see this, however, as on the grounds that the disciples of Jesus *thought* that it happened. The subsequent history of the Church rests on the sheer faith of the first Christians.

What is the matter with this explanation? No one can argue that it is impossible. People are driven by what they believe to be true, whether it is or not. Consider the impact of faith in the Marxist ideal. The problem is that a historical investigation leading to a pronouncement of likely causality requires historical evidence. It will not do to say that such-and-such could have happened. That is conjecture which is the stuff of novels. Novels, especially great ones, incorporate much truth, but they do not masquerade as history. We all know that all manner of other possibilities than are claimed could have happened. Napoleon could have won the battle of Waterloo etc. The historical question is "But what actually happened?"

Even more. Properly historical investigation has to try to account for the fabrication of evidence. Critical assertions, as much as affirmative assertions, need to be looked at as coldly and objectively as possible giving evidence concerning who made this up? when? how? for what purpose? Professor J.N.D. Anderson, author of *Evidence for the Resurrection* (1950) concurs, "Think of the psychological absurdity of picturing a little band of defeated cowards cowering in an upper room one day and a few days later transformed into a company that no persecution could silence – and then attempting to attribute this dramatic change to nothing more convincing than a miserable fabrication... That simply wouldn't make sense."

Where do we go from here? The question of the resurrection of Jesus is pivotal in seeking to answer the question of what caused the huge obvious fact of the origins of Christianity.

The gospels and the rest of the New Testament see this as the supreme factor in kickstarting the new Jesus movement. This event transformed the abject failure of Jesus ending up on a criminal's cross into a movement full of hope and joy with a message to spread to the world.

What is meant by resurrection?

It is important to be clear as to what the resurrection of Jesus concerns. The gospels portray it as utterly unique. It was not reversal of nature: in no way was it a magical transformation of his body back to his normal self, able to live a life as before as a normal human being. This is not a fairy godmother turning a pumpkin into a Prince Charming. The resurrection body of Jesus was a body which bore the scars of death and behaved in unusual ways such as being able to go through a wall into the room.

Nor was the resurrection a way of parading victory over the political and religious forces responsible for his death; it was not a kind of "I told you so" to Pilate and Caiaphas, forcing upon sceptics who Jesus really was. This was no vindication of Jesus before his enemies. As during Jesus' life, miracles were never performed in order to compel people to recognise the action of God. On the contrary, miracles occurred only for those who had faith in God already.

This is an exceedingly important consideration. The fragility of the human capacity for freedom of thought and heart, for thinking for themselves and allowing themselves to be guided by genuine emotions, means that great respect must be given to how the minds and feelings of other people are stimulated. To force people to accept what hitherto of their own freewill, they did not accept, is to violate that respect. If the point of the life of Jesus was to shed light on the love of God thus enabling humans to respond in love, then to use any kind of force would defeat that end.

As practising Jews, the first disciples would have been horrified at the thought that the Messiah could be killed. How could such a person be God's special messenger? To require such incredible re-thinking of traditional habits of mind would require something very special to happen. Attempts to say that the disciples could easily have been hallucinating to believe that Jesus had risen from the dead because that was in line with common thinking are mistaken. Resurrection, so far as it was believed in by most Jews of this period, would not happen till the end of time. The idea of an individual rising before that would not occur to them. There was no known precedent for such a belief. Vermes states, as a Jewish scholar "The most significant peculiarity of the resurrection stories is that they nowhere suggest that the rising of Jesus from the dead was expected by anyone" (1973, p. 398).

Attempts to treat the resurrection as the disciples continuing to believe that Jesus was spiritually alive, because the death of the body could not touch the spirit, would never have been expressed in such terms in those days. Instead, the resurrection of Jesus for the gospel writers was a bold proclamation that this Jesus who had died a horrific death was yet gloriously alive, the physical being taken up into the spiritual. In place of any dualism between spirit and matter, their inseparableness was conveyed, and with it the notion that what happens in this world does matter eternally. We are not just temporary cogs in a machine destined for the rubbish heap.

The overall evidence in the gospels is strong that it was the resurrection of Jesus which kickstarted the whole Jesus movement to become eventually a religion seen as different from all the other religions of the Roman Empire.

What are the consequences of scepticism concerning the gospel evidence?

The edifice built on scepticism towards the gospels conspicuously sheds no light on the most important question prompting the enquiry in the first place. Whilst initial acceptance of the gospels keeps the vehicle of investigation on the road, overall blanket suspicion ensures that scholarship ends up in a cul-de-sac. A major fact of history remains unexplained.

This turns that fact of Christianity, for fact it is, virtually into a miracle itself – it just happened without any real historical cause at all. The Christian church arose which, despite all that has been thrown against it in its long history, including justified accusations of corruption, hypocrisy, naivety, stupidity, violence etc., still stands. Something must account for that, otherwise it was a miracle for which empirical investigation is powerless to aid understanding. This is curiously to stand on its head the apparently rational, anti-miraculous stance of the followers of pure reason, because it leads in the end to having to acknowledge an even greater miracle: that of an explanation-less Christianity.

A dead leader miraculously operates posthumously after his death, instilling in his disciples a false belief that he has risen again when he has not. His followers are so taken over by their new-found faith that they go out to convert an alien world to these strange and clearly impossible musings, for the ancient world just as today knew that dead people do not return to life in any shape or form. Moreover, this miracle-working leader did not use any of the usual agencies for power-driven success: military force, financial manipulation, an educated elite, political control, mass propaganda etc. The first Christians were mostly peasants, without weapons of any kind, wealth, intellectual brilliance, support by those in power, or excellence in marketing skills.

The miracle of Christianity's existence grows the more it is reflected upon. Should not a historian be sceptical of an attempt to portray such a miracle as due to a psychological moment in the lives of such nondescript people?

How have scholars reached such an impasse?

Failure to observe the first two historical principles inevitably has led to failure regarding this third historical principle of providing a comprehensive explanation of the major facts behind an enquiry.

(i) Failing to give initial benefit of doubt to the gospels

To start off by distrusting everything in the gospels, requiring some kind of unchallengeable evidence to reverse that mistrust, is bound to end up in a vicious circle. If nothing can be initially trusted there is no basis for enquiry. Criticism can only take place on the grounds of something which is trusted. So much of the labourious work of scholarship in the search for the historical Jesus has been going round in a circle. If nothing can be trusted in the gospels, then there is no access to any evidence from the gospels. It is just a dead end.

To the objection that not giving initial benefit of doubt does not have to include everything in the gospels, the retort is simply on what grounds is some accepted and other passages not? How do we know, in advance of enquiry, what is to be trusted? The whole point of giving initial benefit of doubt is so that enquiry can begin. Criticism has to have something to criticise; it is basically parasitical.

(ii) Failing to acknowledge the uniqueness of historical events and the dangers therefore of using hindsight inappropriately

A particularly clear example of casting doubt on the gospel evidence for the resurrection through failure to acknowledge this principle is given by the influential arch-critic who used to be a Christian and has now changed allegiance, Bart Ehrman. His book *How Jesus Became God: The Exaltation of a Jewish Preacher from Galilee* (2014), described as a New York

Times Bestseller, seeks to explain subsequent views of Jesus as divine with reference to a common mindset in the first-century Mediterranean world: belief in divine humans, thus linking the human and supernatural spheres. The first of his two chapters on the resurrection of Jesus reads impressively until one realises that it misses the point because it argues from what generally happened to what the gospels claim happened. This fails to accept that history concerns the uniqueness of what happened.

Ehrman bases his argument that the empty tomb visited by the women could be a fiction because of what normally happened to the bodies of crucified people. They were either left to rot to provide an example to others, or they were buried in a communal grave. But what generally happened cannot by itself discount evidence that something unusual happened. The most obvious answer to the questions about an empty tomb and women claiming to have seen the risen Christ is because that is what happened. Why should we doubt it? The discovery in 1968 of Yehohanan's heel, mentioned in Chapter 1, is significant. The skeletal heel nailed to a board by an iron spike was found in an ossuary, or bone box, inside a first-century tomb near Jerusalem. It is an instance of the Romans permitting Jewish burial of a crucified man. This is historical evidence, the significance of which needs to be weighed. It won't do to say that Jesus' burial could not have happened.

The historian has to stick by the evidence given in the sources unless there are good *historical* reasons for doubting it. As Craig notes, "inference to the best explanation" describes a sensible historical approach where we "begin with the evidence available to us and then infer what would, if true, provide the best explanation of that evidence" (in Perman, 2007). In other words, we ought to accept an event as historical if it gives the best explanation for the evidence surrounding it. It is clear from Ehrman's chapters that, despite his array of other possibilities, these only remain at the level of conjecture however many historical facts he includes. The evidence for the empty tomb and the women visiting it cannot be demolished by saying of course it is possible something else happened.

Limits to non-explanation

If the first two cardinal historical principles are not operating, then it leads naturally to failure regarding the third: we cannot know that anything in the gospels is not just made up; our actual reliable knowledge of the historical Jesus is nil. The enquiry is closed.

Why is this result unsatisfactory? The West prides itself on its openness and spirit of enquiry. After all, this is how science has achieved its extraordinary breakthroughs. So why is that same spirit of enquiry unimportant regarding knowledge or ignorance of Jesus? Critics of the gospels have been consciously driven by a laudable commitment to reason. Yet they find themselves in an unreasonable position of having to accept that the development of a major fact which no one can deny just happened of its own accord: that it has no rational explanation.

Basil Mitchell explains in a very careful and moderate academic way what is at stake concerning the resurrection of Jesus:

"'Scientific history', for good reason, does not take [the possibility of the creative power of God] into account, but this methodological restriction on the part of historians does not permit them to claim, on the basis of the evidence, that the resurrection did not happen. At most they can say that, given entirely naturalistic assumptions, some other explanation is to be preferred, or failing that, that it is impossible to settle the question" (1994, p.60).

This kind of acceptance of what we can never know conclusively is wholly acceptable concerning minor matters. Historians do their best concerning incidents such as Napoleon's hat at the battle of Austerlitz (discussed in Chapter 6) or the identity of the young man who fled naked from Gethsemane when Jesus was arrested (Mark 14: 51f), but have to admit they can go no further. To adopt the same attitude, however, to how the French Revolution came about is simply walking away from what history concerns. To conclude an enquiry into the origins of WWI by saying that there is no explanation would not be the comment of a historian. For that is handing an undoubted major true fact into the category of superstition or magic: it just happened.

It is a similar case for the Christian movement and all that followed from it. To fail to offer a plausible explanation for one of the most successful movements in the whole of history betrays an inadequacy of historical enquiry: here is a fait accompli that happened without any apparent reason. This betrays the Enlightenment spirit of enquiry and the obligations of a historian to do all that can be done to recover understanding of the past. Whatever such an attitude is, it is not a rational one. Reason enquires into causes instead of giving the impression that some things, such as the existence of Christianity, just happened.

Chapter 9

Overcoming the Reason/Faith Dichotomy

The purpose of this book has been to open up discussion on the historical evidence for the life of Jesus. In doing this it has been important to distinguish between rational enquiry and faith. Ideology of any kind, religious or not, can interfere negatively with historical study.

Whether Jesus was, or was not, the incarnation of God will always be a matter for people to decide for themselves. People reach this conclusion, or do not reach it, according to their total experience of life and the level of understanding of which they are capable in appreciating the issues involved. It is a matter of faith. This prompts the question: Is there a great divide between reason and faith?

A great divide?

A great divide is often assumed between reason and faith. Lessing's ditch is very much in evidence still. Comments such as "religion is irrational" are frequently voiced. Yet what does such a comment mean? Is it that religious people do not have any reasons for what they believe? That is hard to accept when many people with towering intellects have been, and are, religious. Or perhaps it simply draws attention to the inability of reason by itself to lead to belief in God?

It is important to note, however, that the same reliance on faith attends those who insist on a purely mechanical, science-investigable world view. As Julian Baggini, himself not a religious believer, has pointed out, there is no scientific evidence that there is nothing more to explanation of the world than what science can handle. This point is so critical that I shall give the quotation in full:

"The theologian accepts non-scientific as well as scientific grounds for belief. Much as naturalists may dislike this, there is no easy way of showing this to be in principle irrational. It is not a scientific claim to say that science is the only basis for justified belief. This is rather scientism. Scientism is, however, a philosophical position that needs to be argued for. Science cannot discover that only science leads to truth. Indeed, we should go further and see that a great many scientists – probably the majority – are not scientistic. They do not, for example, base their moral beliefs on laboratory findings, and nor do they devise experiments with which to test the veracity of their partners' love. When judging the aesthetic merit of a poem or a piece of music, they use criteria which are not remotely scientific" (2016, p. 32).

Reason and faith are not so separate as is often assumed. Reasoning is done by human beings who bring their lived experience and feelings to it whether they are pursuing science or not, and whether they opt for religion or not. Similarly, faith unsupported by reasoning is a flimsy affair liable to be overturned according to mood and circumstances.

In practice, firm faith, that is faith which has not merely been conditioned by upbringing or the mindset of the times, always draws on a variety of ways of reaching knowledge in addition to, but including, reasoning. Such ways include imagination, empathy, intuition and "Eureka" moments. The rational and holistic approaches to knowledge meet. There is no deep divide between reason and faith.

The reason/faith divide is close to that so often assumed between thinking and emotional awareness. The over-cognitive approach which has dominated education in the West has tended to leave the emotions to fend for themselves. This is serious because feelings are a major part of people's lives.

It is therefore important to acknowledge that the mind/heart divide is a false one. Not even in the scientific search for objective knowledge can emotional involvement be presumed absent.

Emotional factors enter deeply into a scientist's commitment to pursuing science, for example, in perceiving its worthwhileness, in the importance of striving for accuracy and truthfulness, in willingness to collaborate with other scientists, and in a sense of wonder at the sheer intricacy and beauty of the natural world.

In reality, all thinking is done by human beings with their whole range of possible emotions. Similarly, as achievement in the arts clearly shows, emotionally creative aesthetic work reveals a highly intellectual structure. Bach, for example, was in fact a great mathematician, and one of the reasons for the greatness of his music may well be its foundation in what is mathematically satisfying.

Dogmatism and open-mindedness

I consider that the real divide is between dogmatism and open-mindedness. To settle into a definite viewpoint beyond any chance of challenge-ability spells death to the mind. It is the cardinal sin of so many otherwise worthwhile causes and commitments. Religions offer plenty of examples. So too do political allegiances of many kinds, a straightforward example today being the woke culture which wishes not even to hear anything in disagreement to its own platform.

It is desperately easy for people to become so convinced that they are right that they fail to recognise any possibility of their own limitations in understanding. It is for this reason that discussion and debate, especially with those with whom we may disagree, is so important. A major criticism of the impact of social media has been that it facilitates networks with like-minded people, eliminating conversation with those who think differently. Of course, this is not the fault of social media but of how its potential tends to be used.

Claims to knowledge in all spheres, for us, include accepting open-mindedness to fresh evidence and experience. As rational beings we have to learn to keep conviction and non-dogmatism together; they are not either/ors. This really is possible. See the chapter on "Dialogue" in my book *Making Education Fit for Democracy* (2020).

I have mentioned several times the importance of seeing all our knowledge as partial and provisional. These words were used particularly appropriately in a book by Edward Hulmes titled *Commitment and Neutrality in Religious Education* (1979). He argued that what does damage for religious commitment is holding it dogmatically. This applies to all commitment. By failing to consider the possibility that any of its pronouncements may be mistaken, it closes the door to fresh insight.

Knowledge of Jesus

It is in the sense of comprehensive awareness that we can know a great deal about the historical Jesus whilst at the same time pursuing the search for ever-increasing understanding. Awareness of mystery can and must be coupled with a reasonable level of certainty. Schweitzer was indeed right in exclaiming that Jesus comes to us as one unknown, quoted in Chapter 2, in the sense that our minds are incapable in themselves of appreciating fully what is infinitely beyond their capacity. This constitutes a major reason for open-mindedness. Understanding of the historical Jesus will never be complete; it is always work in process.

It does appear that the Jesus portrayed in the gospels was not dogmatic. Openness of mind and heart was much to the fore in the way Jesus taught and lived. The whole point of the parable mode of teaching was to entice people to think for themselves imaginatively. He did not tell them what to believe, but invited reflection.

Moreover, time and again, Jesus is shown as wanting to get beneath the labels by which people, then as now, are mostly known. Thus, he refused to be drawn into being pro- or anti-

Roman, "Give unto Caesar the things which are Caesar's and unto God the things which are God's" (Matthew 22:21). He asked very pointed questions when his family turned up without warning, wanting to stop his activity: "Who is my mother and my brethren?" (Matthew 12:48). In the parable of the Good Samaritan, the labels of Priest, Levite and Samaritan were discarded as irrelevant in favour of the simple term neighbour (Luke 10: 25–37). All the time he was asking people to relate to other people as persons and not by the umbrellas under which they were usually counted and ignored.

This astonishing openness to human beings as people was central to his message of caring for all and not just for some. He even prayed for forgiveness for those who were crucifying him. Even in a situation of obvious violence and hostility he still did not see enemies but people.

Relevance of Jesus for today

One would have to be very bold and optimistic to say that the world today is not urgently in need of this message of putting people first instead of causes or ideologies. The causes themselves need to be broken down into their human aspects, just as ideologies need rigorous criticism and debate based not on preconceived hostility but in an attempt to reach real understanding.

I return to a point made in Chapter 1 that, if Christians could make more effort in trying to understand the human Jesus, this might increase their powers of discernment for understanding and acting upon current problems. This in itself could perhaps encourage those of other persuasions and religions to do the same. Followers of the Taliban need, for example, to be reminded of the Allah whom they believe they are serving. Taj Hargey, Imam of the Oxford Islamic Congregation, has noted: "Virtually everything the Taliban stands for is in clear contravention of the Qur'an and is a betrayal of authentic

111

Islam" (2021). He argues that violence, subjection of women and so forth are not in the Qur'an, so why are the Taliban supporting them in the name of Islam?

The interpretation of Jesus which emerges from the gospels needs first to be challenged on historical grounds. All the scholars pursuing the Quests have been insistent that this is so: that their work is an historical, not a philosophical, pursuit. The problem, however, has been in the understanding of history which many have tended to assume. The secularist mindset of the modern age, emerging in the West from the Enlightenment, has presumed that History is a purely empirical form of investigation. It can only take account of what potentially is available to scientific study. This means that it is barred from interpreting any events, or teaching, to anything other than a human source; divine intervention has to be ruled out, for this world view holds that either the divine does not exist or that if it does it is irrelevant – just as Epicureanism taught. See discussion in the Appendix on this.

I have tried to show that this understanding of history is inadequate on rational grounds. It ignores three specific foundational historical principles. The gospels should be approached in a truly historical manner. If they are, then the quest for the historical Jesus can move into acknowledging that we can know a good deal about Jesus as a historical person and that faith, or not, in him should take account of that historical knowledge.

Finally, I am hoping that this study of the historical Jesus may have helped to give some confidence in the capacity of reason and faith to work together and point in the same direction. They do not have to be at loggerheads. Indeed, that is not a rational position. I would rather put it that we should all be as rational as possible, and that this can relate comfortably with faith provided that the way in which the faith is held is open enough to ongoing enquiry.

Appendix

Further Information about the Scholarly Quests

Three quests?

The Quest for the Historical Jesus is generally seen to have been in three phases, the first starting in the late eighteenth century, the second in the 1920s and the third, which is still continuing, in the 1970s. This division, however, is criticised by some. Hilde Brekke Moller considers that "the generalisations overshadow considerable diversity ... marking shifts in history by specific dates, years or events is bound to oversimplify" (Moller, 2017, p. 32). She discusses other ways of mapping research into the historical Jesus such as Clive Marsh's division into eight quests defined by content and methodology which are not mutually exclusive and do not fit easily into specific time periods. These he names: The Positivist Quest, The Romantic Quest, The Form-Critical Quest, The Quest of the Non-Jewish Jesus, The Traditio-Historical Quest, The Existentialist Quest, The Jewish-Christian Quest and The Postmodern Quest (Moller, p. 36). In many ways such analysis is more accurate. Gerd Theissen and Annette Merz in *The Historical Jesus: A Comprehensive Guide* summarize the quests in five phases (1998, pp. 1–13). However, the three-fold quest terminology is so widely used that it seems necessary to use it too, but with a note of caution, as Moller herself does.

Form Criticism

Formgeschichte was a term coined by Martin Dibelius in 1919 who, alongside Bultmann, practised it. The two scholars worked independently but reached similar results. It claimed to offer a scientific method by drawing on literary and sociological research on the handing down of oral tradition in various societies. It drew attention to typical features found in the handing down of hymns, laments, proverbs, laws, tales, myths etc. These were then related to their context, their *Sitz Im Leben*, their setting in real life. This might be in worship, education, entertainment, politics or laws etc.

This method had been used to great effect by Hermann Gunkel in seeking to understand the sources and history of Genesis, the Psalms and the Prophets. K.L. Schmidt in his study of the Synoptic Problem in 1919 noted that these gospels were composed, apart from the Passion narrative, of circulating independent units of oral tradition: *pericope*.

The method has been criticised on many grounds, for example, for ignoring or downplaying the role of the evangelists in the writing of the final gospel. There is, moreover, a conspicuous lack of any certainty that the short pure forms reconstructed by Form Criticism ever actually existed. The method also gave much stress to the creativity of the early Christian communities without again much real evidence for that creativity. So, the whole thing could be seen as arguing in a circle.

Of course, Form Criticism has yielded many insights; it was over-focussing on it that was the trouble. Also, behind it lay the Positivist desire for some kind of scientific, objective certainty which in reality was, and is, a pipe dream. Scientific methodology can only achieve its reliable results when applied to the purely physical domain. Enquiry concerning Jesus is hugely more than a purely physical study.

The influence of Bultmann

It is interesting that the extraordinary importance Bultmann placed on the believer's faith caused him eventually to minimize the importance of what happened regarding Jesus' historical life. Although his early work had inspired the second quest, his later work virtually brought it to an end. He became convinced that the gospels should be de-mythologized, replacing references to the supernatural with comments on universal human values. This was in line with what David Strauss had taught.

John Muddiman in an article on Form Criticism in *A Dictionary of Biblical Interpretation* summarized the impact of Bultmann's work in a quite damning way: "His combination of form-criticism and neo-orthodox fideism and a Christian existentialism, effectively excluded concern with Jesus from the agenda of biblical interpretation for a whole generation of critical German scholarship" (1990, p. 242).

Gains of the third Quest?

Vermes's most famous book was *Jesus the Jew* with its subtitle *A Historian's Reading of the Gospels* (1973). Molle considers that this book "describes the majority of subsequent Jesus research and sums up the self-perception of many contemporary Jesus scholars. Attention to the Jewish Jesus and a historically-focussed search are marked features of third quest rhetoric" (2017, p. 224).

Meier has spoken of seven notable gains as compared with the other quests: (i) The third quest has an ecumenical and international character. (ii) It clarifies the question of reliable sources. (iii) It presents a more accurate picture of first-century Judaism. (iv) It employs new insights from archaeology, philology, and sociology. (v) It clarifies the application of criteria of historicity. (vi) It gives proper attention to the miracle tradition. (vii) It takes the Jewishness of Jesus with utter seriousness (1999, pp. 459–487).

I agree with most of these but I don't think that two of them apply. (v) ignores certain foundational historical principles and (vi) fails to take seriously enough the material in the gospels which is associated with miracle. The question of reliable sources and the application of criteria of historicity has not been clarified for all scholars. In both these areas residue from earlier challengeable assumptions is still powerfully at work.

Impact of Epicureanism

I will add here an interesting postscript to the overall reason for the problems facing the Quest. Wright has spoken of the Epicureanism which he regards has become the implicit understanding of a majority today, at least in the Western world. Enlightenment Deists were thoroughly Renaissance men looking back to the ancient classical world for inspiration. They were impressed especially by the teaching of Epicurus as embodied in the great poet Lucretius who lived in the first century BCE. "The brooding Epicurean [i.e., Lucretius] inspired the youthful Voltaire and the mature Holbach, and his memory sustained the dying David Hume"(2019, p. 12). Wright notes that for Epicureans "the gods don't care, and they won't judge, so how we behave is up to us, and death dissolves us into nothingness."

This philosophy did not deny the existence of the gods, but saw them as entirely separate from the real world of nature. According both to Epicurus and the Deists. God exists but has nothing to do with the running of the world. God may have created the world but is not involved in any way in it; there is no supernatural. The world exists on its own and can be understood entirely without any religious input at all. This does seem to be a fairly accurate summary of how the secularised West does see religion, not necessarily dismissing it completely but seeing it as quite irrelevant to living.

Wright comments that "this was the view of a small minority in the classical world, but it has now become extremely widespread, and he offers a reason. The well-functioning Epicurean needed money, a nice vineyard, and compliant slaves. But with the new skills developed in Europe it seemed possible at last that a whole society might attain the goal" (p. 28). This theory of Wright's is relatively novel, but it offers an interesting perspective on the modern world and why scholars can expect to encounter such difficulties in dealing with historical religious material such as the gospels provide.

The quests began as an Enlightenment project and, until its legacy and ongoing Epicureanism is challenged in this respect, its future will remain precarious.

References

Anderson, J. N. D. 1950 *Evidence for the Resurrection* Inter-Varsity Fellowship, London

Armstrong, Karen 2019 *The Lost Art of Scripture: Rescuing the Sacred Texts*, Bodley Head, London

Armstrong, Karen 1993 *A History of God*, Ballantine, London
Baggini, Julian 2016 *The Edge of Reason: A Rational Sceptic in an Irrational World*, Yale University Press

Baggini, Julian 2020 "The genius of ambiguity" in Holland

Bauckham, Richard 2006 *Jesus and the Eyewitnesses: The Gospels as Eyewitness Testimony*

William B. Eerdmans, Grand Rapids, Michigan

Bloom, Harold 1994 *The Western Canon: The books and school of the ages*, Harcourt Brace & Co., New York

Boldt, Andreas D. 2016 *The Life and Work of the German Historian Leopold von Ranke*, Peter Lang, Oxford

Booker, Christopher 2009 *The Real Global Warming Disaster: Is the Obsession with 'Climate Change' Turning out to be the Most Costly Scientific Blunder in History?* Continuum London
Bornkamm, Gunther 1956 *Jesus of Nazareth*, Fortress Press, Philadelphia

Breisach, Ernst 2007 *Historiography: Ancient, Medieval, and Modern*, Third Edition, University of Chicago Press, Chicago

Brown, Dan 2003 *The Da Vinci Code*, Doubleday, New York

Bultmann, Rudolf 1921 *Die Geschichte der synoptischen Tradition* trans1976, *History of the Synoptic Tradition*, San Francisco, CA Harper, San Francisco

Carrier, Richard 2014 *On the Historicity of Jesus*, Sheffield-Phoenix, Sheffield

Caesar, Julius *Gallic Wars* trans. W.A. McDevitta & W.S.Bohn 1869, Harper & Brothers, New York

Coggins, R.G. & Houlden, J.L edit.1990 *A Dictionary of Biblical*

Interpretation, SCM, London

Crossan, John Dominic 1991 *The Historical Jesus: the life of a Mediterranean Jewish peasant*, T & T Clark, Edinburgh

DeConick, April 2007 *The Thirteenth Disciple: What the Gospel of Judas Really Says*, Continuum, London

Denning, David 2016 "Do Extraordinary Claims Require Extraordinary Evidence?", *Philosophia* 44 No.4 December

Dunn, James D.G. 2003 *Jesus Remembered: Christianity in the Making Volume 1*, William B. Eerdmans, Grand Rapids Michigan

Dunn, James & McKnight, Scot 2005 edit. *The Historical Jesus in Recent Research*, Eisenbrauns, Winona Lake, Indiana

Dunn, James D.G. 2013 *The Oral Gospel Tradition*, William B. Eerdmans, Grand Rapids Michigan

Dunn, James D.G. 2019 *Jesus According to the New Testament*, William B. Eerdmans, Grand Rapids Michigan

Dworkin, Ronald 2006 *Is Democracy Possible Here? Principles for a New Political Debate*, Princeton University Press, New Jersey

Ehrman, Bart D. 2014 *How Jesus Became God: The Exaltation of a Jewish Preacher from Galilee*, HarperOne, New York

Evans, Richard 2020 *The Hitler Conspiracies*, Penguin Books, London

Eve, Eric 2016 *Writing the Gospels: Composition and Memory*, SPCK, London

Geary, P. 1978 *Furta Sacra: Thefts of Relics in the Central Middle Ages*, Princeton, New Jersey

Habermas, Gary 2005 'Resurrection Research from 1975 to the Present: What Are Critical Scholars Saying?", *Journal for the Study of the Historical Jesus* Vol. 3.2 pp. 135–153

Hanson, R.C.T. & Hanson A.T.1989 *The Bible Without Illusions*, SCM, London

Hardy, Henry 1997 *Isaiah Berlin: The Proper Study of Mankind*, Chatto &Windus, London

Hargey, Taj 2021 "As a Muslim I'm horrified the BBC gave a

platform to an apologist for the Taliban", *Daily Mail* August 24

Hengel, Martin 1991 *The Pre-Christian Paul*, in collaboration with Roland Deines, SCM, London

Hill, C.E. 2010 *Who Chose the Gospels? Probing the Great Gospel Conspiracy*, OUP, Oxford

Holland, Tom edit. 2020 *Revolutionary: Who Was Jesus? Why Does He still Matter?*, SPCK, London

Hulmes, Edward 1979 *Commitment and Neutrality in Religious Education*, Geoffrey Chapman, London

Hunt, Lynn 2018 *History: Why it matters*, Polity, Cambridge

Irenaeus of Lyons *Against the Heresies*, edit F.R.M. Hitchcock, 1916 SPCK, London

Kasemann, E. 1954 "The Problem of the Historical Jesus" in *Essays on New Testament Themes* trans W J Montague SCM, London 1964

Khalidi, Tarif 2020 "Worshippers of revolution: Islamic perspectives on Jesus", in Holland

Lapidge, Michael 2003 *The Cult of St. Swithun*, Clarendon Press, Oxford

Larsen, Matthew D.C. 2018 *Gospels Before the Book*, Oxford University Press, Oxford

Lataster, Raphael 2015 "Philosophical and Historical Analysis of William Lane Craig's Resurrection of Jesus Argument", *Think* 43:10 Spring pp. 59 ff

Lataster, Raphael 2016 "It's official: we can now doubt Jesus' historical existence", *Think* 43:15 Summer pp.65–79

Lessing, G. 1777 *Lessing's Theological Writings* trans H. Chadwick 1956, Stanford University Press

Litwa, M.David 2019 *How the Gospels Became History: Jesus and Mediterranean Myths*, Yale University Press, London

Longenecker, Bruce W.; Parsons, Mikeal Carl 2014 *Beyond Bultmann: Reckoning a New Testament Theology*, Baylor University Press, Texas

Lounissi, Carine 2018 *Thomas Paine and the French Revolution*, Palgrave Macmillan, London

Lüdemann, Gerd 2004 *The Resurrection of Christ: A Historical Inquiry*, Prometheus Books, New York

Luff, Rosemary Margaret 2019 *The Impact of Jesus in 1st century Palestine: Textual and Archaeological Evidence for Long-standing Discontent*, Cambridge University Press, Cambridge

McGilchrist, Iain 2009 *The Master and his Emissary: The Divided Brain and the Making of the Western World*, Yale University Press, Newhaven Connecticut

Meier, John P. 1991 *A Marginal Jew: Mentor, message, and miracles*, Doubleday, New York

Meier, John P. 1999 "The Present State of the 'Third Quest' for the Historical Jesus: Loss and Gain" *Biblica* Vol.80, No.4, pp. 459–487

Metzger, Bruce 2003 *The New Testament, its background, growth and content*, 3rd revised and enlarged edition Abingdon Press, Nashville Tennessee

Mitchell, Basil 1994 *Faith and Criticism*, Clarendon Press, Oxford

Moller, Hilde Brekke 2017 *The Vermes Quest: The significance of Vermes for Jesus research* T&T Clark, Edinburgh

Morison, Frank 1987 *Who Moved the Stone?*, Zondervan Academic, Grand Rapids, Michigan

Mournet, Terence C. 2005 *Oral Tradition and Literary Dependency*, Mohr Siebeck, Tubingen

Muddiman, John 1990 "Form Criticism", *A Dictionary of Biblical Interpretation* edit R.G. Coggins & J.L. Houlden SCM, London

Neill Stephen and Wright, Tom 1998 *The Interpretation of the New Testament 1861–1986*, Oxford University Press, Oxford

Nineham, D.E. 1963 *Saint Mark: The Pelican Gospel Commentaries*, Bloomsbury Publishing, London

Paine, Thomas 1794 *The Age of Reason* ed. Kerry Walters, Broadview Press, Peterborough 2011

Perman, Matt 2007 'Historical Evidence for the Resurrection', online under the 'Desiring God' logo September 12

Porter, Stanley. E. 2000 *The Criteria for Authenticity in Historical-Jesus Research: Previous Discussion & New Proposals,* Sheffield Academic Press, Sheffield

Reimarus, H.S. 1774–8 *Apology or Defence for the Rational Worshippers of God,* published in part by G. Lessing, trans R.S. Fraser and ed C.H. Talbert under *Fragments,* Fortress Press, Philadelphia 1970 Robertson, Ritchie 2020 *The Enlightenment: The Pursuit of Happiness 1680–1790,* Penguin Books, London

Robinson, James M. 1959 *A New Quest for the Historical Jesus,* SCM, London

Sanders, E.P. 1977 *Paul and Palestinian Judaism,* SCM, London

Schweitzer, Albert 2006 *The Quest for the Historical Jesus: A critical study of the progress from Reimarus to Wrede,* 3rd Edition translated W.B.D. Montgomery, A.& C. Black, London

Schweitzer, Albert 1912 *Paul and His Interpreters,* translated W.B.D. Montgomery, A & C Black, London

Stendhal, Krister 1963 "The Apostle Paul and the Introspective Conscience of the West", *The Harvard Theological Review,* Vol. 56, No. 3 Jul, pp. 199–215

Spencer, Nick 2016 *The Evolution of the West: How Christianity has Shaped our Values,* SPCK, London

Spencer, Nick 2020 "Jesus Christ, game changer", in Holland

Stern, Fritz (ed.)1973, *The Varieties of History,* Vintage Books, Penguin Random House, New York

Strobel, Lee 2016 *The Case for Christ: A Journalist's Personal Investigation of the Evidence for Jesus,* Zondervan, Grand Rapids, Michigan

Talekau, Pallavi; Jyotrimayee, Nayak, & Harichandan, S. Utkal University Vanivihar, *UNIT I Concept of History,* Bhubaneswar, Odisha, India,

Tarnas, Richard 1991 *The Passion of the Western Mind: Understanding the Ideas that have Shaped our World View,* Penguin Random House, New York

Theissen, Gerd & Merz, Annette 1998 *The Historical Jesus: Comprehensive Guide*, trans John Bowden, SCM, London

Thorsteinsson Runar M. 2018 *Jesus as Philosopher: The Moral Sage in the Synoptic Gospels*, Oxford University Press, Oxford

Tomalin, Claire 2002 *Samuel Pepys: the Unequalled Self*, Penguin Random House, New York

Van Dam, R. 1992 *Saints and their Miracles in Late Antique Gaul*, Princeton, New Jersey

Vermes, Geza 1973 *Jesus the Jew: A Historian's Reading of the Gospels*, Collins, London

Watson, Brenda 2004 *Truth and Scripture: Challenging Underlying Assumptions*, Aureus, St Brides

Major, Vale of Glamorgan

Watson, Brenda 2018 "An unbelievable myth: the invention of Jesus", *Think* 50:17 Autumn pp. 51–56

Watson, Brenda 2020 *Making Education Fit for Democracy: Closing the Gap*, Routledge, Abingdon, Oxford

Watson, Peter 2000 *A Terrible Beauty: A History of the People and Ideas that shaped the modern mind*, Weidenfeld & Nicolson, London

Williams, Peter J. 2018 *Can We Trust the Gospels?*, Crossway, Wheaten Illinois

Wittgenstein, Ludwig 1951 *On Certainty*, Blackwell, Oxford

Wright, N. T. 2019 *History & Eschatology: Jesus and the promise of natural theology*, SPCK, London

Index

Abaelard 84

Acton, Lord 9

Alfred the Great 87f.

Alexander the Great 55

Anderson, J.N.D. 99

Archeological evidence. 20, 90,
    104

Armstrong, Karen 13

Arts 86f, 91f, 108f.

Atheism 1f,.10, 24; 48f, 60

Bach, J.S. 109

Baggini, Julian 4, 107f.

Bauckham, Richard 21, 65f.

Benefit of doubt: Chapters 4 & 5

Berlin, Isaiah 67-69

Bible 2; 22-24

Blair, Tony 12

Blomberg, Craig 55f; 57f; 61; 62

Bloom, Harold 7

Booker, Christopher 85f

Borg, Marcus 94

Bornkamm, Gunther 18

Both/and cf. either/or 92

Boyd, Gregory 53; 60, 76

Boyes, Roger 90

Brown, Dan 4

Bultmann, Rudolf 17-20; 72; 113-
    115

Caesar, Julius 28, 89f

Campbell, Alastair 12

Campbell, James 41

Carrier, Richard 13, 59

Charles 1 69

Church. 6, 61f, 71f., 78ff, 102

Christianity, 1f,.
    ignorance of: Chapter 1,
        Chapter 8 esp. 101f.
    fact of Christianity Chapter 8
    origin of 102
    seen as evangelisation. 71f

Colston Edward 29

Columbus, Christopher 90

Confucius 6

Conjecture cf evidence 1f., 78,
    81f., 99, 104f

Craig, Wiliam Lane. 61, 95, 104.

Criteria for authenticity. 68f, 74-
    79
    coherence/consistency. 75; 81,
        87-89
    historical plausibility. 75, 106
    Palestinian environment. 75
    multiple attestation 75f.
    dissimilarity 76-79
    embarrassment 77

Critical affirmation. 45f., 103

Criticism of gospels
    agenda-controlled 47, 54; 62f
    authorship of gospels 54; 57f.

community documents. 54; 60-62; 71-73

conspiracy theory. 54, 63f.

dating 53f ;55-57, 60f.

discrepancies 54; 58f

orality 54; 64-66, 69, 73f

supernatural. 54; 59

Crossan, John Dominic. 94

Dam, Raymond Van. 50

Dawkins, Richard. 6

Deism. 49; 116 see Epicureanism. 116f.

Dibelius, Martin. 113f

Diderot. 29f.

Disagreement & need for dialogue 83-6 109

Discernment, need for 11, 111f. cf.Jesus & Christianity. 5-8

Dogmatism versus open-mindedness. 52, 105f, 109-111

Dunn, James 21, 23, 65f. 73, 77f, 94,

Dworkin. 42f.

Education. 3 86f., 89, 108

Ehrman, Bart 68, 76, 103-5

Einstein, Albert 86

Either/or. cf. Both/and. 92, 110

Emotional awareness. 86, 108f false separation of cognitive and affective capacities Chapter 9

Enlightenment. Chapter1,15f., 22, 26, 45, 49, 92, 106; 112, 116f

Epicureanism. 49; 112, 116f.

Evans, Richard. 91

Eve, Eric 47, 72

Evidence 36-39, 97f. historical evidence. 67 81f., 95 - 105, 112

Explanation of Major Facts. Chapter 7 & 8

Facts. 30f., 85-87 need for interpretation 30, 51f., 80, 95 faith & evidence. 50f., 98

Forgiveness and identity. 40, 110-112

Form Criticism 17f., 71-74

Freewill 10, 100f.

Funk, Robert. 21f.

Gandhi , Mahatma 5, 6

Geary, Patrick 52

Gender. 2, 88f

Gospels. 1f, Chapter 1, 101f.

Greenleaf, Simon 58f. 97f

Gunkel, Hermann 114

Habermas,m. Gary. 96

Hamman, J.G. 33

Hanson R.C.T. & A. T. 22

Hargey, Taj 111f.

Hegel 35

Heidegger, Martin 17

Hengel , Martin 39

Hill, C.E. 63f; 71; 75

Hindsight. Chapter 6, 96f, 103-5

History, nature of: 24 - 26,
   Chapter 3. and psychology.
   95ff

Hitler.Adolf 5, 17, 57, 69, 90f.

Holbach 116

Holistic awareness cf.logic 91-3,
   108
   concern for completeness and
      comprehensiveness 89-91
   collaborative enquiry - search
   for what is common. 111f.

Holland, Tom 4,

Hulmes, Edward 110

Hume, David. 70, 116

Hunt, Lynn. 35; 41; 80f; 83; 87, 91

Hunter, Tom. 49

Hurtado, Larry 97

Ideology, world-view, faith 1f,
   Chapters 1, 8 & 9 111f.

Impartiality 68f., 83

Inclusivism 86
   Jesus;'s attitude towards
      identity 110f.

Irenaeus of Lyon 63

Islam. 46, 111f.

James 58

Jesus Seminar. 21f., 41, 79, 94f.

Jewishness of Jesus. 20-22, 77, 115

John 56

Josephus 37

Judaism 20f. 115

Judas Iscariot. 63f, 75

Kasemann, Ernst. 18. 78

Khalidi, Tarif 46

Lantfred 51

Lataster, Raphael 4; 12f; 50f; 59;
   78

Levi 58, 66

Lessing' Gottfried 15, 19, 27, 34,
   48, 107

Lucretius. 116

Luff, Rosemary, Margaret 20

Ludemann, Gerd 37-9, 95f

Luke 56,58

Mandela, Nelson 5, 40

Marie Antoinette. 29

Marsh, Clive 113

Mark 56f. 58, 72, 106

Mary 58, 63

Marx, Karl 35

Matthew 56, 58, 66, 111

McGilchrist, Iain 92

McKnight, Scot 23

Meier, John 19f; 27f; 34; 115

Merz, Annette 113

Miracle. 24f. 50-2, 54, 59f. 100,
   115

Mitchell, Basil. 56f; 83f; 105

Moller, Hilda, Brekker. 113, 115

Morison, Frank 98

Moore, Captain Sir Tom. 82

Muller, Julius. 61

Mudiman John 115

Myth. 61, 114

Mystery, need for acceptance of
16f., 110

Napoleon 5, 67f., 81, 83, 87f, 99,
105

Neill, Stephen. 21

Nineham, Dennis 72

Obama 41f, 80f,

Ongoing nature of enquiry. 91-3,
109f.

Orwell, George. 39

Paine, Thomas 6, 12, 29; 59f; 69

Parable 110f.

Good Samaritan 8, 111

Paul 13,, 37f, 56, 95-7

Pepys, Samuel 43f.

Perrin, Norman 76

Peter 37f., 58, 77, 95f.

Philip. 58

Porter, Stanley E. 75; 78

Positivism cf. scientism 26, 34, 47,
108, 108, 114

Postmodernism 31

post-truth 9, 84

Provisional and partial nature of
knowledge. 33, 46f. 91, 110.

danger of expecting certainty
30f.

Quests. 1; Chapter 2; Appendix

Ranke, Leopold von 25f; 28; 34f.,
62, 72, 91

Reason 1f, Chapter 1, 22, 24, 44,
102, 106

reason/faith dichotomy. 2, 18-
20, 27, 34, Chapter 9

Reimarus, Hermann Samuel 15f;
19, 36; 47f; 59

Relevance of Jesus today. 8-13;
111

Religion. 10, 12, 109f, 116

abuse of 5 -8

Renan, Ernest 20, 37

Resurrection of Jesus. 36-39;
Chapter 8.

Rhodes, Cecil 70

Robertson, Ritchie 49

Robinson, James 18

Sanders, E.P. 21

Scepticism. 1f, Chapters 1 & 2,
34, 76

Schleiermache, Friedrich 36

Schmidt, K.L. 114

Schweitzer, Albert. 14, 16f, 97

Science. 18-19, 105

cf. history 27f., 31-35, 68, 85f.
112

cf. faith. 26; 34;47. Cf,
McGilchrist. 92

cf. religion. 18, 49

cf. Anthropogenic Global

Warming (AGW) 45f. 85f..

limitations of 92f.

Scientism. cf positivism 26, 34,
108f.

Shakespeare, William. 10, 28

Stendhal, Krister 96f.

Strauss, David 15f; 18, 37, 115

Strobel , Lee 53; 61; 63, 98

Subjectivity 30, 82-85, 94, 107-9

impossibility of objective
enquiry. 74ff

bias 82-85

Synoptic Problem. 56, 73f., 114

Tarnas Richard 11

Theissen, Gerd. 113

Thomas. 63

Tiberius 55f.

Tillich, Paul 45

Tomalin, Claire 43f.

Trump. Donald 41f., 48, 80f

Tutu, Desmond 40

Uniqueness of historical events.
Chapter 6, 103-5

Value. 84, 115

Vermes, Geza. 21, 98, 101,   115

Voltaire 116

Watson, Peter 7

Wagner, Richard 69

Williams, Peter. 55f; 64f

Wittgenstein 46

Wokism. 39, 49, 70; 83-85; 90,
109

values. 11

Worsley, Lucy 30f

Wright, Tom 21; 32f; 35; 38; 61,
116f

CHRISTIAN ALTERNATIVE
BOOKS

THE NEW OPEN SPACES

Throughout the two thousand years of Christian tradition there
have been, and still are, groups and individuals that exist in
the margins and upon the edge of faith. But in Christianity's
contrapuntal history it has often been these outcasts and
pioneers that have forged contemporary orthodoxy out
of former radicalism as belief evolves to engage with and
encompass the ever-changing social and scientific realities. Real
faith lies not in the comfortable certainties of the Orthodox,
but somewhere in a half-glimpsed hinterland on the dirt track
to Emmaus, where the Death of God meets the Resurrection,
where the supernatural Christ meets the historical Jesus,
and where the revolution liberates both the oppressed and
the oppressors.
Welcome to Christian Alternative... a space at the edge where
the light shines through.
If you have enjoyed this book, why not tell other readers by
posting a review on your preferred book site.

Recent bestsellers from Christian Alternative are:

Bread Not Stones
The Autobiography of An Eventful Life
Una Kroll
The spiritual autobiography of a truly remarkable woman
and a history of the struggle for ordination in the Church of
England.
Paperback: 978-1-78279-804-0 ebook: 978-1-78279-805-7

The Quaker Way
A Rediscovery
Rex Ambler
Although fairly well known, Quakerism is not well understood.
The purpose of this book is to explain how Quakerism works as
a spiritual practice.
Paperback: 978-1-78099-657-8 ebook: 978-1-78099-658-5

Blue Sky God
The Evolution of Science and Christianity
Don MacGregor
Quantum consciousness, morphic fields and blue-sky
thinking about God and Jesus the Christ.
Paperback: 978-1-84694-937-1 ebook: 978-1-84694-938-8

Celtic Wheel of the Year
Tess Ward
An original and inspiring selection of prayers combining
Christian and Celtic Pagan traditions, and interweaving their
calendars into a single pattern of prayer for every morning
and night of the year.
Paperback: 978-1-90504-795-6

Christian Atheist
Belonging without Believing
Brian Mountford
Christian Atheists don't believe in God but miss him: especially
the transcendent beauty of his music, language, ethics, and
community.
Paperback: 978-1-84694-439-0 ebook: 978-1-84694-929-6

Compassion Or Apocalypse?
A Comprehensible Guide to the Thoughts of René Girard
James Warren
How René Girard changes the way we think about God and the
Bible, and its relevance for our apocalypse-threatened world.
Paperback: 978-1-78279-073-0 ebook: 978-1-78279-072-3

Diary Of A Gay Priest
The Tightrope Walker
Rev. Dr. Malcolm Johnson
Full of anecdotes and amusing stories, but the Church is still a
dangerous place for a gay priest.
Paperback: 978-1-78279-002-0 ebook: 978-1-78099-999-9

Do You Need God?
Exploring Different Paths to Spirituality Even For Atheists
Rory J.Q. Barnes
An unbiased guide to the building blocks of spiritual belief.
Paperback: 978-1-78279-380-9 ebook: 978-1-78279-379-3

Readers of ebooks can buy or view any of these bestsellers by clicking on the live link in the title. Most titles are published in paperback and as an ebook. Paperbacks are available in traditional bookshops. Both print and ebook formats are available online.

Find more titles and sign up to our readers' newsletter at
http://www.johnhuntpublishing.com/christianity
Follow us on Facebook at
https://www.facebook.com/ChristianAlternative